Lydia

Shirley Nelson

ISBN: 1456413007
ISBN-13: 9781456413002
LCCN: 2010918018

SEACOAST REGION
OF
NEW HAMPSHIRE

Perspectives '76 (p.A14)

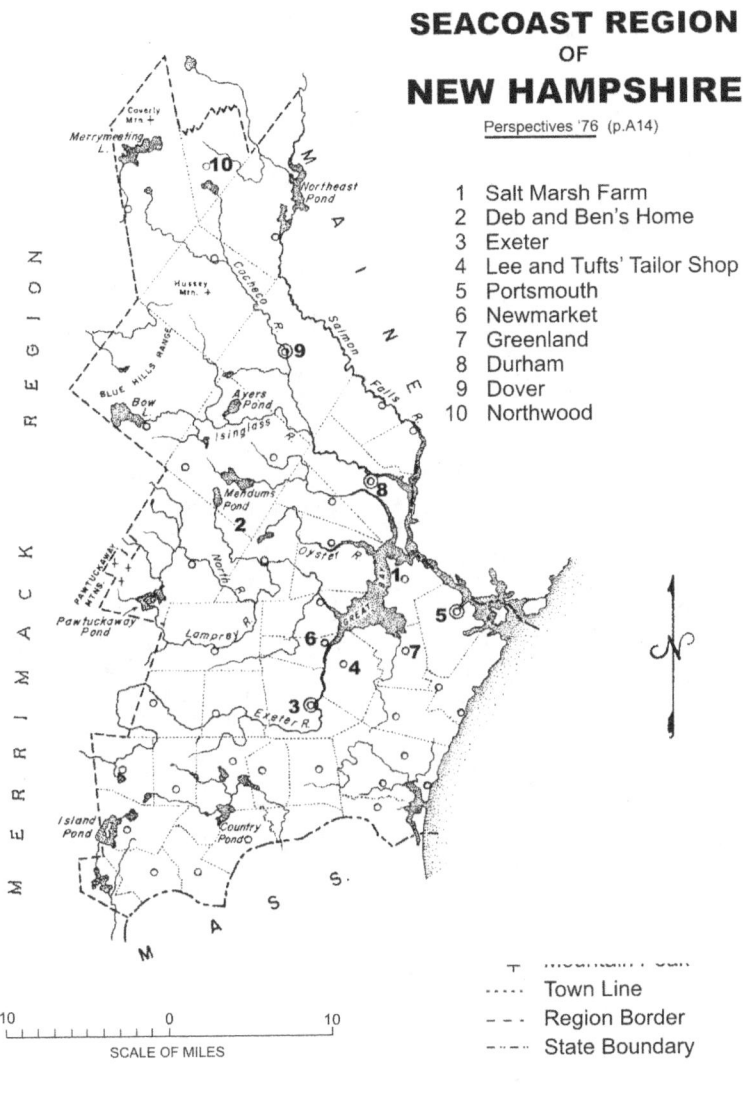

1 Salt Marsh Farm
2 Deb and Ben's Home
3 Exeter
4 Lee and Tufts' Tailor Shop
5 Portsmouth
6 Newmarket
7 Greenland
8 Durham
9 Dover
10 Northwood

Town Line
Region Border
State Boundary

10   0   10
SCALE OF MILES

Map of
YORK COUNTY, MAINE

Dedication

This book is for my father, Frederick K. Durgin, who was concerned all of his life that his forebears should not be forgotten. Thanks to you, Dad, Lydia has been remembered for nearly 80 years.

Foreword

Some of my happiest early memories are of the times my father told the family about his forebears. Sooner or later, "Old Dr. Henry Tufts" was mentioned. He was a colorful ne'er-do-well who stole horses, broke out of jails many times, and had many women in his life. He was born in Lee, New Hampshire, in 1748 and died in Limington, ME, in 1831. Henry was used as a frequent example of how I was <u>not</u> to behave as I grew up.

As I grew older, learned more about the history of our country, and thought about Henry's ways, I became curious about his first and only legal wife, Lydia Bickford Tufts. The more I read about Henry in the histories of several New Hampshire towns as well as the history of Limington, Maine, the more I wondered about Lydia. She gave birth to six of his children, yet he could never have really lived with her and still accomplished all of the bad things he claimed, and is reputed, to have done.

During Lydia's lifetime, women could not own property of any kind, could not vote, and had little to say about matters that affected their own lives. They were chattels of men.

Then there was the question of Lydia and Henry's second child, a boy who did not grow up with Lydia, but with Henry's older brother. What could have happened? This story contains answers to the many questions that occurred to me about Lydia's life during the nearly 80 years I have known only a little about her.

Several people are to be thanked for their support and interest in Lydia's story: Dr. Eugene Scruggs, of Florida Presbyterian Homes, read chapter by chapter as they issued from my word processor and provided valued suggestions; Dr. and Mrs. George Laird Hunt, also from FPH, read the completed manuscript and provided many supportive suggestions; Old friends Ruth Bridges Ayers and Barbara Storer, from Maine, read the manuscript and gave very helpful feedback about local descriptions; Mildred and Jerry Heinicke, FPH friends and neighbors, proofread the manuscript and used their knowledge and skills of publishing with a computer at just the right time. Most of all, my dear husband of nearly 60 years encouraged, encouraged, and encouraged some more. Thank you, each and every one.

Chapter 1

Earliest Memories

1742 ~ 1754

My name is Lydia Bickford Tufts and this is my story. It is a true story, based on events that really happened. Dates can be found in the records of churches and the histories of Towns where the events took place.

My father was named Joseph and called "Ben" after his Grandfather, Benjamin Bickford. Ben's Grandfather had received a King's Grant of 30 acres located on the road between "Bloody Point" and Greenland, N. H., in the Plantation of Oyster River. The Grant was dated 1694, and my father, Ben, always talked proudly about the line of inheritance from his grandfather to his father to himself. The Bickford land was located on Great Bay, a large shallow body of water that stretches south from the Piscataqua River. Our house was a small Cape Cod style with two big rooms downstairs and two small rooms up. The two downstairs rooms were about the same size, with each taking up one half of the first floor space.

In the center of the house there was a huge chimney with a fireplace and a brick oven facing into each first floor room. There was one smaller fireplace in one upstairs room. The fireplaces were the only heat in the house, and the downstairs ones were where all the cooking was done. The house fronted to the south with the low back roof facing into the north winds that blew cold in winter months. The north side of our house had no windows. The south windows caught the rays of the sun, both summer and winter.

The southeast end of the house faced Great Bay, and from our front door and windows we could see a dock that jutted out into the water of Great Bay at the end of the Road to Greenland. The Greenland Road ran from the dock on the eastern end, toward Greenland Village in the west. It passed in front of the house and beyond into a marshy meadow. Although others called our area "Bloody Point," probably after some long ago Indian battle according to my father, we called our place "Salt Marsh Farm" because of the water soaked soil that lay in front of the house and on the opposite side of the Greenland Road.

My mother's name was Margery. Her family connections remain a mystery to me. If she had any brothers or sisters, they were never part of our lives. Whenever my mother was asked about her family, she would say, "That's not important for you to know." And she would change the subject, usually to tell me how badly I had done a chore or an errand. I stopped asking about such family ties after a few attempts.

Dennis was my older brother, about ten or more years older than I. Next in age, Daniel, was two or three years older. Daniel always did what Dennis told him to. My mother used to say that she had been "Churched," or accepted into the Newington Church as a member, in May of 1742. That was the same day I was Christened, so that became my birthday—May ninth, 1742. Whenever my brothers teased me, I would retort

"I was Christened on May ninth, and you weren't Christened until two weeks later, on the twenty third of that month, so there!" I'm not sure what that proved, but it seemed to end the sneers from them.

We all went barefoot in the summer, to save the precious leather shoes we wore in winter, as well as to enjoy the coolness of the mixed salt and fresh water in the marsh around the house. The tufts of stringy grass that grew in the wet soil cut into fingers and toes, and so each spring we had to "harden up" our feet. That was no problem because everyone did it.

My dog, "Buster," was my constant companion, and knew all of my secret desires. He seemed to consider himself my protector from any evil or danger. Until I reached the age of five or six, he was taller and much bigger than I was, and so if he stood in front of something he thought bad for me, I would have to go all around him to get to it.

"There is one place you and Buster must NOT go," my father said often, "and that is onto the dock, and that is final." My father was the person in charge of our family. He would plan the work

3

of the day each morning and give jobs to each of us. My older brothers usually worked outside together, and I tried to help my mother inside the house and also in the kitchen garden, just outside the back door on the western side of the house.

Buster always seemed happy when I said to him, "Let's go snake hunting." He pricked up his ears and even looked as if he was smiling whenever he heard me say those words. Still smiling and wagging his tail, he would watch as I chose a long, tough stick to poke for the prey. We would go to where snakes might be lurking—between the stones in a rock wall or in small holes in the ground. Buster would watch with all attention as I poked the stick into holes, and whenever a snake grabbed it and I could get the snake out of the hole, Buster was ready to grab that old snake just behind the head and shake the life out of it, growling loudly as his tail wagged in circles at the same time. We could be sure of praise from my father whenever we took a dead snake to him, because snakes, ever present around the barnyard, were dangerous to have near where there were baby chicks, ducks, and turkeys. Babies of those kinds of animals were easy food for the snakes, and so the snakes lived close by their food supply.

The barn, in addition to a place for the farm animals to shelter, was used to store hay and other grains like oats, rye, and wheat. The barnyard also held the henhouse. One of my earliest daily chores was to gather the eggs each morning for my mother. "Egg time, Lydia," she would say, and I would find the egg basket and head for what turned into a daily test of wills, that is, until I found a way around the hen pecks. For a long time, my hands and arms were covered with scabs and sores that were shaped like triangles. Those sores were made by the "Broody" hens, the ones that did not want to give up their eggs, but wanted to set on them in the nests until the eggs hatched into chicks. The hens knew how to peck small hands and arms with an added pinch that not only hurt, but also broke the skin and caused the sores and scabs. One day, the meanest of the old hens pecked me hard on my arm, and I lost my temper. I smacked her in the head with my fist and knocked her right off that nest. After rolling around on the floor until she got her senses back, she started for my bare feet and legs. I was able to get the eggs, but soon lost the contest with that old biddy, and retreated in shame from the henhouse. After that, I wrapped an old rag around my egg-fetching hand and arm. When my father asked which old hen was not producing enough eggs, I was quick to point to that old broody one, and the chicken dinner that followed in a few days was very tasty.

Another chore, a more enjoyable one, was to feed oats to my father's beautiful horse, "Honery Steed," usually called just "On'ry." Although his name meant "big, stubborn, strong horse" he was my best friend in the barn. When my father said,

"Give On'ry a treat, Lydia," I was glad to fill the wooden grain measure with oats and climb up into On'ry's manger. He knew what I had for him, and so he welcomed me. When he was done with his treat, he would let me feel his soft muzzle and lips. While he was eating, I could observe why he was said to have "...a hard mouth." His teeth did not go way to the back of his mouth like mine did. He allowed me to feel way back in the side of his mouth to the hard, flat bones there. It was obvious how he had found a way to take the bit part of his bridle and hold it with those hard bones so that the bit did not pinch his tongue and force him to obey the signals from the reins. Therefore, On'ry obeyed his rider whenever it suited On'ry.

On'ry was my father's constant companion whenever he was away from home, which seemed to me to be very often. The horse had been trained to be in battles, and he took my father, who was a Captain in our town's "Sons of Liberty," to the training they had every month. On'ry knew how to march proudly with his neck arched and his front legs rising so that his knees nearly hit his breast while his back legs danced in time with the drum beat. On'ry also knew how to move sideways suddenly, or to "shy," which could unseat a rider less experienced than my father. That was why no one else in the family was allowed to ride him, and why riding him became my dearest wish. Sitting tall in the saddle was the way I always remembered my father, with On'ry prancing away to a "meeting."

One day, after the many times I had begged to do so, my father boosted me up to On'ry's back for a ride. Father and On'ry were about to leave for one of the "meetings," and so On'ry was all saddled and bridled. I was not prepared for the military type of saddle, with the big hole in the middle. My small rear end went right down through that hole in the saddle and ended up on On'ry's backbone.

There I was, with my legs waving uselessly in the air, yelling in frustration, and my older brothers and mother, who had gathered to see my father off, were laughing until they wept. Finally, my father, with kind patience in his eyes and voice said,

"Come, my girl, to ride tall in the saddle you must use your head and your legs, straighten up your spine, and BE somebody!" I followed his instructions, and soon I was sitting tall like he did. Before long, he allowed me to ride On'ry and guide him myself, and my dear On'ry never shied or unseated his small rider.

Until I was nearly into my teen years, I enjoyed the peaceful life on our Salt Marsh Farm. The whole family worked together throughout the seasons of the year to provide for our needs. There was a time for planting crops, for harvesting them, for shearing the sheep and for providing for the winter months. There were sociable times, too. Every Sunday there was "Meeting" to attend, with a long sermon, and a pot luck meal for which all the women brought their "best dish."

Sundays meant that there was an exchange of news among all our neighbors, some who lived near us and some who lived far away, too. There was always talk about the Sons of Liberty meetings my father went to, and I learned that those meetings included practice with guns, and marching, as well as information about what the Indians and the Privateers were doing that might threaten our lives and farms. It was finally evident to me that my father's frequent activities away from home were to protect us and our beloved Salt Water Farm. He was called "Captain," by most of the men at Meeting, and sometimes he was asked to speak and inform the entire group about either Indian or Privateer situations that could be dangerous.

By the 1750's the Indians had gone north into the mountains and were not considered as dangerous as the Privateers. Those men were sea-going, and made raids on farmers and tradesmen who were going by boat from Great Bay to the Piscataqua and down-river to Portsmouth to trade for necessities such as sugar, molasses, whale oil, and other things that could not be made on the New Hampshire farms. If the farmers defended themselves, they were sometimes injured or killed outright. Thus far, the Privateers had not raided on land, but The Sons of Liberty were the only defense the farmers had against them. It came to me that my father's warnings to keep off the dock into Great Bay were not to be taken lightly. He often warned other families with docks in Great Bay to keep children and pets off their docks, too. The Privateers lurked near the coastline, and could spy small children to kidnap for ransom, or worse.

1754 came along, and on May ninth my mother announced that I would soon be known as the "Old Maid" if I didn't soon begin courting. I was not sure what she was talking about, and asked her what "Old Maid" and "courting" meant. She replied,

"Silly thing, it means that you will soon get married and have some babies and keep house for them and for a husband. BUT, child, you must stop being so lazy and learn to keep a house, a garden, to spin and to weave, and to do all the other chores a woman must do." Thinking about it all, I decided that being twelve years old was not very much fun, but I set about to learn all I could from my mother about keeping a home.

My mother was not a patient teacher, and after a very short time of my trying to do a task she had given me, she would give up and say,

"You'll never learn; you're too lazy! Go and play with Buster." So I never really learned much about cooking meals, or about spinning, weaving, or sewing. I could hoe the weeds out of the kitchen garden, rake hay, make shocks of the oats and rye grain stalks, and prepare the flax to be soaked in the flax pond. I learned the out of doors chores from my older brothers, who were a little more patient than my mother, but still not very positive or ready to praise my attempts to learn. I heard them tell their friends at Meetings on Sundays not to come courting me because I was too dumb and lazy to really learn to do anything.

When my father was home, which seemed to be less and less of the time, my life was more pleasant, and when I did something right he always praised me and said, "Good girl." More and more often, "You and Buster keep off the wharf," were included in his directions. In spite of my frustrations trying to please my mother and older brothers, I thought I was meant to live on the Salt Marsh Farm all of my life, and that my days would improve when I was able to do better at pleasing them all.

Late in that year of 1754, my dream of living happily on the Salt Marsh Farm came to an end. One day in November, three of my father's friends from the Sons of Liberty came riding into our yard with very sober faces. The youngest man looked as though he had been crying. When I greeted them from the kitchen garden beside the house, they asked to talk with my mother, so I went inside the house and asked her to come out to talk with them. Her face fell when I told her who they were, and she said,

"This is the day I have dreaded for years," as she went out the door. I did not hear what was said, but soon she was crying, and as she came back inside, she would not speak to me. The men rode away without another word to me either. My mother told me to fetch the boys from the field, which I did, and then I heard that my father was dead. A big change came to my life, and that is why the year 1754 is a dark memory to me.

Chapter 2

1754 - 1770

Daily life on our salt marsh farm was not happy without my father. There was much bickering about nearly everything—what the tasks for the day should be, whether a crop was ready for harvest, who should do what job and where. Nothing satisfied everyone, and last of all opinions to be considered was mine. Dennis's favorite name for me was "Idiot Girl." Daniel, when he spoke to me, got my attention with, "Numbskull." My mother could seem to find any number of words that meant "Lazy Bones," for me.

Dennis always said, "Why do I bother to explain that? You wouldn't understand if I did." I learned to say very little and to keep out of sight of everyone as much as possible.

Keeping out of my mother's sight was not hard to do. She was busy "courting." She was away from home more than my father had been. Someone had to get the meals for my brothers, who worked outside for long days, and argued most of the time. I learned to make gruel from oats and to fry bacon and eggs in the fireplace, and I managed to make a very poor loaf of bread in the brick oven. Making soap and candles were done with other women, and so I was able to bring home some soap and candles from the "Bees" for our use. Keeping the kitchen garden and gathering the eggs were the least of my worries. I was accustomed to those chores. During the year after my father died, I became thinner and very tired all the time. I wondered how so many wives and mothers lived for so long. I decided that being a homemaker was not for me, and the urging by my brothers to "go a'courtin'" was a lot of poor advice, I thought, so I stayed home to rest.

It was about that time when my brother Dennis, a rare kind look on his face, said he needed to talk to me to explain some things about who owned the Salt Marsh Farm. I listened carefully. Dennis said, as usual, "You probably won't understand this, Knucklehead, but these days the oldest son inherits all property, the land, the house and everything in the house and on the land. I think you should be looking harder for a husband, because I've found the girl I'll marry, and when that happens, you'll have to move out of my house, and Mother'll have to move out, too. Women have nothing to say about inheritance, and what the oldest son of a family wants is what goes. I don't want you living here anymore. You can never own anything; even the pots and pans'll be mine. You can't vote, either, so in spite of what you say, you don't have a vote in who will follow our father as Captain of the Sons. Don't bother to complain about this to anyone, because no one'll listen; it's the way it is. What you need to do is learn to be a good housekeeper, find a man who will put up with you, and have lots of his babies." He began to laugh, and I began to understand that I had a problem.

Bickford relatives came often to call, and they tried to help my brothers and me. Aunt Deborah and Uncle Josh Babb, my father's sister and her husband, tried to talk to us and help us adjust to our lives without our father and his magnificent horse, On'ry. I missed my friend in our barn that liked the oat treats I used to give him, but the only one I could really share my loneliness with was Buster. However, I did not have much time to spend with Buster. We couldn't hunt for snakes anymore, because I was too busy with keeping the house and getting the meals. I knew Buster missed our romps as much as I did.

One day, my Uncle Benjamin and Aunt Deborah Bickford came and asked to talk with my mother. Uncle Benjamin was my father's older brother, and he and Aunt Deborah had been married many years. They had grown children who lived in the area, too, and while I called them all "Aunt" and "Uncle," some were really cousins. They had taught me about making soap and candles at the Bees.

At the time Aunt Deb and Uncle Ben came to see my mother, it was 1756. We had been without my father for nearly two years. My Aunt and Uncle were getting older, and they needed some help to keep their big house and busy life going. Aunt Deb said to my mother,

"Could you spare your Lydia to come and live with us and be our girl? We would care for her as if she were our own. She is getting to the "Old Maid" stage, and will need to find a man to marry her soon. We have a nice room that she could have, and we could spare a few pence a week for her allowance. Of course, we will give her good food and teach her to run a good household."

My mother seemed pleased with the idea, and replied,

"Lydia can't seem to learn much, and she is lazy as the day is long. If you want to take her off my hands in spite of that, I'd be relieved. With Dennis's plans to marry soon, she's getting to be a burden I don't need."

That decision made, I packed my belongings into a grain bag, patted a sad goodbye to Buster, and was off with my Aunt and Uncle in the back seat of their wagon with hope in my heart for better days to come.

My Aunt Deb and Uncle Ben lived inland a little, in a big two story "Garrison" house on what we called the upland. There was no tough grass to cut bare toes. Rather, the grass was soft on bare feet in the spring time. A Garrison house was a sturdy one, two and a half stories, with a huge chimney that occupied the center of all the levels. It had been built during the tough Indian raid days, and had a seven foot tall fence of pointed stakes all around the outside. The house itself was built of solid logs that had been squared off so that no bark showed, and the square beams were laid on top of one another.

The second story jutted out over the front of the house, and there were sliding boards here and there called "gun ports" where the settlers could aim their rifles at Indian invaders. The solid walls protected those inside from arrows, and the windows all had wooden shutters to protect the glass. First floor windows had shutters inside as well as outside, so there was double protection. As I learned about the house, I found out there was a "smoke chamber" in the attic where meat and vegetables could be cured by the smoke from the fireplaces for use later on. There was also a "root cellar" that could be reached from the cellar of the house, and in addition to preserving vegetables for use in the winter, it had been a hiding place for people when the Indians attacked.

I was given my own room on the second floor, and for the first time I could have my own things as I wanted them. The room had a bed, a cabinet for folded clothes, a table and a chair. Beside the bed, there was a table for a candle, too. My Aunt, when she showed me that candle table, mentioned reading in bed, and cautioned me to be sure to remember to put out the candle when I went to sleep. I confessed that I could not read, and she listened with kindness to my rather long list of "can't do's."

My Aunt Deb was a kind and patient teacher. She did a lot of showing instead of telling and blaming. Soon I was responsible for cooking breakfast. I learned to put the oatmeal in cold water on the fire at night so that it would be ready in the morning, and I learned to fry the bacon until it was crisp in the spider, or frying pan, with three legs. The cooking utensils were iron, and there were cranes with trammels on each, to make the cooking easier by adjusting how close to the fire the pots were hung. The brick oven near the kitchen fireplace was big enough to bake several loaves of bread at once, and I learned how to put the bread dough to rise and then to bake it. My bread went from being made "by guess" –good sometimes and bad a lot of times–to being called "by gorry, that's good!" My Uncle praised me for going from "by guess to by gorry" so fast! He loved to say things that were fun, and so that was how he told me he liked my bread all of the time.

My Aunt and Uncle were both gentle and positive with my schooling, and soon I was reading, writing, and doing some figuring. Those were skills I would use all of my life, and I remember the joy of learning that came to me through my kind Aunt and Uncle. By the time of my 15th birthday, I could spin both linen thread and wool yarn. It amused me that we used a "walking" wheel and stood up to spin wool into yarn for knitting or weaving, and we used a small wheel with a foot pedal while sitting down to spin flax into linen thread. "Stand up to make yarn, sit down to make thread," was a little ditty I said to myself. Slowly, my Aunt Deb taught me to weave with both wool and linen. My favorite became using both to make what we called "Linsey woolsey," which we then sewed into shirts for the men and frocks for the women. My allowance could be used to buy pretty fabrics, which I chose with my Aunt's help, and I learned to sew pretty frocks to wear to socials. In many ways, the years with my Bickford relatives were the happiest of my life.

In addition to Sunday Meetings, my Aunt and Uncle encouraged me to go to all the frolics, or social occasions, with other young people. There was a close-knit neighborhood nearby, and nearly every week there was a quilting bee, or a barn dance or some other social event for young people. Some of those events were seasonal, like the Husking Bees in the fall after the corn had been harvested.

The dried corn cobs, with the shucks still on, would be stacked in the middle of a barn floor, and the young folks would sit in a circle around the stack of corn. The point of the "Bee," was to remove the husks, or shucks, and leave the dried corn kernels on the cobs to be further processed later. Usually, the boys sat on one side and the girls on the other side. Whenever a boy discovered an ear of "Indian Corn," with red or brown kernels, he would have the choice of which girl on the other side of the stack of corn to kiss. Of course, there was much hooting and whistling while he chose the girl and planted the kiss—on the mouth, yet! As the stack of husked corn got smaller, the stack of corn husks got bigger, and for some reason, the number of ears of "Indian Corn" increased. I have given much thought to that fact, but I've never reached any firm conclusion.

During the colder months, the soap-making Bees, candle-making Bees, and Quilting Bees were held. No matter what kind of Bee or Frolic, there was always a meal to accompany the occasion. When the women met for Bees, the men usually were working elsewhere, maybe at a barn-raising, but they appeared for the meal. Then boards would be placed on saw horses— tools men used to do carpentry work—and the food, every woman's best dish, would come off the fire. With my Aunt's help, I learned to make delicious "Hotch Potch," or meat stew, for such occasions. I also learned to make Indian Pudding, a dessert of corn meal and molasses, that was popular.

I loved the parties, but I remembered the lessons learned on the Salt Marsh Farm, and I never found a boy who could match the memories of my father. The smiles that lit up his eyes as well as curved his lips, and his gentle ways seemed not to be found among the boys I met. I had looked in the polished steel mirror in my room, and I knew that I had very blonde hair and very blue eyes. When I was dressed in my good clothes, my Uncle Ben would say, "You are a very pretty girl, Lydia." I suspected that the boys agreed with him, but I tried never to let a boy think that he was "a-courting" me.

As the years passed for me in this happy way, my Aunt Deb's health began to fail. She was soon spending much of the time in bed, with hot coals from the fireplace in the long handled metal warming pans to keep her comfortable. Her four daughters, all of whom lived nearby, were Sophronia, the oldest, Maybelle, Sarah, and Nancy the youngest. They often helped me with the care of their mother. They had their mother's patience to show me ways to help her sit up without hurting her sore joints; to feed her nourishing drinks when chewing became hard for her, and they sat with her often so that I could ". . . have a social life." Each told me, in her own way, that they knew what it was like to be young, considered to be pretty, and yet very unsure of the future. No one said it outright, but long ago I had passed the early years of Old Maidship.

I turned twenty the same year that Aunt Deb died. We all missed her gentle ways and wise advice. Long ago, my own mother had gone out of my life with hardly a "goodbye." She left the salt marsh farm soon after I did, and very soon after that she disappeared totally from the area. Off to be married, I supposed.

Sophronia, on behalf of the four sisters, came to the Garrison house one day soon after Aunt Deb had been buried. She seemed to have weighty matters on her mind, and so I sat quietly while she got ready with them.

"Lydia, we have been very pleased with the way you helped our mother through her last days, and we want you to know that if you can see your way clear, we would like you to stay on and see our dear father through his last days, too. They were so close in thinking and together so many years that none of us can imagine that he will live very long now that Mother has gone."

"Aunt Sophie, I'm pleased that you and my other Aunts liked the way I tried to help your mother. She and Uncle Ben have been like mother and father to me, too, and I will be glad to stay on with him as long as he wants me to." So, it was decided. My "Aunts," who were really cousins, all continued to help me in many ways. They took me with them for "Birthings," which every woman in those days needed to know how to do. They continued to sit with Uncle Ben whenever I had a Frolic to go to, and they helped me learn how to care for that nice old gentleman. I ignored the Old Maid talk, and I continued to look at the few men of my age who were not married with my father in mind. My Uncle Ben, too, always came out on the top of any comparisons I might make with the men I met at socials. The young men were all too short, or too fat, or too loud, or reminded me of my brothers and their name-calling, and none of them ever smiled with their eyes as well as their mouths.

As Uncle Ben's health failed, he decided that I needed some help caring for the big house. He got a housekeeper to cook and clean and keep the kitchen garden, and I attended to my Uncle's needs. We moved his bed to the first floor, and a cot was added to his room where I could spend Uncle Ben's many restless nights. He became forgetful, and needed someone to know where he was all of the time. He was always gentle, but could get lost and not be able to get himself into a familiar place. At first, he would lose his way in the neighborhood; then it was in his house. He needed constant attention toward the end of his life. His daughters and I did not begrudge time spent with him, for he was always so gentle and would do our bidding. However, it was a constant concern of ours. All four of his daughters were kind to me in many ways. They insisted that I continue to attend as many of the social events as possible, and they kept me up-to-date on what event was coming next. All of them had children who were old enough to be in the social swing of things, and they knew all that was going on in the surrounding towns. In May of 1769, I turned 27, and that was really "Old Maidsville." I refused to consider it seriously. I was busy with Uncle Ben's day-to day life, and the socials I attended were sort of true "frolics" and not very serious activities, I thought.

The summer of 1770 was a long, hot summer. Uncle Ben, it seemed, could not let go of life. He had lived 8 years without Aunt Deb, when we had thought it would be only a short time he would live without her. I was getting weary; his four daughters were getting weary; yet he lived on. His mind was gone, and there was nothing left, even the way he looked, that would remind us of his former self. His frustrations were beginning to show in his words and deeds, and he was not the gentle, passive man he had been a year or so earlier. The doctor gave us an herb to help him sleep a lot. He still needed someone to sit with him, and so my four "Aunts" and I took turns and split up the days and nights to keep him company.

Sophie, my favorite, was due to sit with Uncle Ben on what turned out to be a very special Husking Bee night in September of 1770. Sophronia sent word that she was attending a birthing, and Nancy would take her place. Nancy was not always as prompt as Sophronia, and so I was late getting to the Husking Bee.

Chapter 3

Henry

It was no sin to arrive late to the Husking Bee, and as soon as I had assured everyone that Uncle Ben still lived, and that I had brought an Indian pudding for the potluck meal, we settled down to the evening's task of husking corn. There was only a small pile of shucked ears of corn and another small pile of the husks in the middle of a big circle of young people. However, I failed to notice the strange fellow on the opposite side of the piles.

Chatting with my girlfriends, I exchanged gossip items and jokes. Soon, there was a big hoorah and much whistling on the other side of the barn floor behind the piles of corn husks and ears. Around those piles came the tallest, darkest, handsomest man I had seen since my father died. He held up an ear of Indian corn and said,

"I claim the right to kiss the prettiest girl here who has the cerulean eyes." I did not know the word "cerulean" meant blue, so I was surprised when he stopped in front of me. He reached down for my hand to help me stand up for his kiss, and when he did, he smiled—with his eyes twinkling. My knees grew weak, and I welcomed his firm grip around my waist as he gave me a long and thorough kiss. He bowed and thanked me for the kiss. Unheard of! I sat down and he went back to the men's side of the circle. When we stopped the husking to eat, he was by my side. He claimed the entire Indian pudding, saying it was the best he had ever eaten.

Before the night was over, I knew that I was in love. His name, I found out, was Henry Tufts. His reputation had traveled ahead of him, and I knew that he was a notorious scapegrace. I never knew just how he did it, nor did I really care, but he came into possession of at least 12 ears of Indian corn that night, and he kissed me thoroughly for each one.

For the next six months, until spring, he was at my side every time I went anywhere. He was at Meeting on Sundays in the small Meeting House, he was at every frolic I attended; he danced every dance that I did, and with me. He was a marvelous dancer—so light on his feet!

My Bickford relatives were all shocked and saddened by this courting that I seemed to be encouraging. Each of them in turn tried to talk with me and to discourage me from continuing the meetings. Uncle Ben passed to his reward, which was neither unexpected nor terribly sad. We celebrated his life at Meeting.

Again, my Bickford relatives stepped up to counsel me as they had when my real father died. Aunt Deborah and Uncle Josh sat for a whole afternoon to tell me all about the things Henry Tufts had done that were very "shady." Uncle Josh said,

"Do you know, Lydia, that he made Sally Nall pregnant last year? He tried to deny it, and when the Court nabbed him, he paid her off with $10.00 on the sly so that he wouldn't have to marry her or support her and her baby? He's just plain bad news." They retold all of Henry's thieveries that they knew about, and they told me about all of his bad friends, too.

Henry had confessed to me that he was not perfect, and he also told me how much the gossip, some of it untrue, he said, hurt his feelings. I could not help taking his side in my thoughts, although I tried not to argue with my Bickford relatives, for I knew they meant well. "You're getting to be a complete Old Maid," I told myself, "and you also need to keep in mind that your Bickford relatives like your nursing and birthing help. Aunt Sophie is a good nurse, and she taught you to be a good one, too. With the next generation coming along, and the present one getting older, the Bickfords don't want to lose you."

Aunt Sophronia sat down with me one day, and she reminded me that while I was nearly 28, Henry was only 21 years old, a mere lad with many wild oats yet to sow. She had a point, and I knew it. She also had a point when she reminded me how disappointed Aunt Deb and Uncle Ben, as well as my father, would be if they knew of my "friendship" with Henry. Sophronia's husband, Uncle Abner, was an Elder of the Meeting I attended.

She said, "Lydia, you need to know that the Elders are talking about bringing forth a "shunning" of you. They do not want to do it, because of the recent death of your Uncle and the loss of your home, but Henry Tufts is NOT the proper husband for you, and we all feel that very strongly." A Shunning is not a nice thing to see. When one of the Meeting members did something opposed to the principles of the other members, they would neither look at nor speak to the one who erred, either at Meeting or in every day life. The Shunned person was made very miserable, and if that happened to me, there would be no one whom I could talk to about anything. That made me think very carefully. I thought a lot about what Sophronia had said. But then, I closed my eyes and saw the smile that came into Henry's eyes and lighted up his whole face when he looked at me, and I heard his kind voice talking about how beautiful I was with my "cerulean eyes," and I weakened. All the Bickford family warnings were in vain.

By the time the first hay mowing came along in July, 1771, I knew that I was totally hooked, and I also knew that I was carrying Henry's child. My birthing experiences had taught me to count months, and I knew there would be a Christmas baby in our lives. One day that July Henry came walking jauntily along the lane as I was using the bull rake. A bull rake is a Heavy oak wooden rake used by one person to make rows and then stacks of dry hay to gather and haul to the barn for storage. It was a heavy tool and a hard task, but I had done it for years.

Henry took the rake out of my hands and said, "My girl, that is not a tool for a woman to use, and that is not a woman's work."

It was time for me to tell him about my being with child, and so I did that day in that hayfield. He professed surprise, but pledged to ". . .make it all right." We talked about the disapproval of the Bickfords, which he knew about, and the disapproval of the Tufts family, which seemed to be more his mother than his father. Henry said, "All right, my cerulean beauty, do not give it another thought. I shall discuss this with my father, and he will help us to get started in life as a married couple, I know."

We were married by the Preacher in September. Henry had suggested the Constable, but I wanted a Preacher. We found one in Exeter who married us, and we settled into a loving marriage. I was so happy—happier than I remembered ever being. It seemed a hundred years, not just one, since that Husking Bee when I first saw Henry Tufts. Most of my thoughts were plans about what we would do when our child joined us. Henry was a good provider, and I never questioned where the money he gave me to run the house came from. He always gave me compliments on my ways with our meager expenses, and I lived in a bubble of pure bliss.

When our son, Simeon, was born in December of 1771, my life and dreams were complete. "Simeon" means "Man of God," I think, and it seemed we were set out for a God-directed life, as members of the Meeting in Exeter and the with the new friends we could make there.

Simeon was a contented baby, crying only when he was hungry or needed a change of his under cloths. When he lost his "baby colorings," his eyes became as blue as the sky—"truly cerulean," Henry said. His hair, when he lost the baby fuzz, was very blond, and so Henry talked about his "Two cerulean beauties." Before long, Simeon could look at me, ". . .straight in the eye," and the expression in his eyes and on his face could tell me a whole story. In a way, Sim and I began a mother-son love that never faded. It waxed and waned, but never went away.

Henry was not at home when a knock came on our door one cold night in late February, 1772. It was the Constable. Henry had been accused and found guilty of stealing from the collections of our small Exeter Meeting. He was being held in the Exeter Jail. I wept many tears, hoped for the best, and waited. I knew I had to think of Simeon now, and if I became too distraught, my breast milk, his only food, would disappear and so I could not dwell on problems that were too upsetting.

A few nights later, a faint tap came on the door and when I opened it, there stood my naked husband the father of my Simeon.

He said, "Ah my cerulean beauty, let me in before I freeze to death."

I let him in, warmed him up by the fire, and found some clothes for him to put on.

No sooner was he dressed than he said. "Lydia, my love, they have arrested the wrong man, but I must be away before they find me to torture me further. I will be in touch with you anon."

He left us again, without money again, and without a word from him about where he had been, where he was going, or when he would be back. My father's advice when I had faced the challenge of the military saddle came back to me. "BE Somebody! Use your head and your legs and sit tall in the saddle."

After a few days, the landlord came to collect the rent for the cottage. I had no money. Neither was there much food in the cupboard. I had enough firewood for only a few more days. He was kind, but he had no answers or much help for me, and he did not know anything about Henry or where he might be. As Landlord Forbes advised, I took Simeon on my hip and walked to my nearest Bickford relatives. They listened, shook their heads, and told me they could not afford to take me and Simeon in but maybe Aunt Sophronia, who had always spoken highly of my help with her parents, could find a home for me and my son.

Aunt Sophronia and Uncle Abner took Simeon and me to live with them for a while. However, their feelings toward me had changed, and that was very plain to see. I tried to feel at home with them and to help them as much as I could. Try as I might, I never seemed to really please them with cooking or other kinds of work. Their answers were short if they spoke to me at all, and they told bad stories of what they heard about Henry. I learned what "Shunning" could be like.

During all of these hard months, I shared my sadness with Sim, and he seemed to know my thoughts as I whispered them to him while I rocked him to sleep at night or at nap time. He would look at me with a very serious look in his knowing blue eyes and put his little hands on my teary cheeks as if to say, "I'm sorry, Mama."

Henry's mother and father lived nearby in Lee; their family had all grown up and left home. Their oldest son, Thomas, lived with his new wife in Northwood, and Eliphalet, their second son, had enlisted in the Continental Army that was being formed from the Sons of Liberty groups in all the small Towns. Henry Sr. sent word to me that he needed help with his business as a Tailor. He had more work than he could do making uniforms for the new Continental Army. Thinking about my father's words so Long ago, once more I took Simeon on my hip and I walked to the little cottage in Lee, full of hope and energy that I could "BE somebody," and provide for myself and for my son Sim in the future. It was June, and Simeon Tufts was six months old. Henry Tufts was, I hoped, alive somewhere.

Chapter 4

1772 – 1775

It was a lovely late June day as Simeon and I walked along the Exeter-Lee Road to the little house where Henry's parents lived. The sun was shining, and the hayfields were fragrant with drying new-mown hay. Mr. Tufts' message had not been urgent, and so I had taken time to say farewell to my Bickford relatives—at least the few who would still speak to me—and I strolled slowly along the Road, with Sim on my hip, encouraged about the future for him and me.

As we passed the Adams farm, I heard the familiar bleat of sheep being shorn. That bleating always made me wonder if the sheep objected more to the losing of their wool coats, or to the being deposited without apologies onto their rumps for the job to be done. At any rate, the sheep always objected to being shorn with a most sorrowful bleating.

As we strode along, I sang little tunes to six month old Simeon that I made up on the spot. He chuckled in pleasure, I thought, whenever I sang,

"Georgie, Porgie,
Puddin' and pie,
Kissed the girls,
And made' em cry."

I sang it over and over, but with a different tune each time so that he wouldn't get bored. He did not know, of course, that the ditty was making fun of the English King, George III, who was coming up with all the taxes that made such trouble for us.

After we had walked for about two miles, the Tufts house came into view. It was on the inland side of the road, in upland rather than marshland like my "heart's home." It looked much like my first home. It was a Cape Cod, 1½ story cottage, with two windows on each side of the front door—a "full Cape", we called it. In front of the house, there was a long hitching bar about three or four feet high for tying up horses that had brought customers to Mr. Tufts' tailoring business. On a little knoll behind the house was the barn. It was where the Tufts' animals were kept, hay and flax were dried, and the wagon was parked. The barn overshadowed the house by more than a story and was set end to the road with a double door on rollers facing the Road. Noticing with surprise the hitching bar full of horses, some of which were harnessed to wagons, I thought, "Mr. Tufts must really need help with so much business."

As soon as we were near enough to the house to hear the sounds coming from it, I knew that there was trouble within. Simeon's face began to pucker up in fear as we heard a high piercing keening like what I had heard at Irish Wakes. I hurried to the house to see what was going on inside. By the time we reached the door, Sim, frightened by all the loud noise, was crying.

Over the many voices, I heard Henry's father's voice: "Thank God, here is Lydia. She will know what to do."

As I searched for familiar faces in the crowded tailoring room, I saw Henry's mother, Mary, who was making the loud keening sound. Beside her was my Henry, with a very bloody left thigh. He was holding it, standing on his right leg, and trying to stop the generous flow of blood, as it spouted rhythmically from his thigh. I handed my Simeon to a pair of outstretched arms, and went to my husband's side.

"Please, everyone, go to the other room and give space for me to help my Henry." I found a chair and lowered him into it. He was very pale, and for once, he did not say anything about "cerulean." I took his pulse, and it was slow, and I noted that the spurts of blood from his thigh matched the beat of his pulse. A major blood vessel must have been cut. I asked for something to cut the leg of his breeches, and I used a piece of the cut breeches to tie tightly above his wound, which I could now see was very deep indeed. I asked for some warm water and vinegar and a clean cloth. The flow of blood began to ebb, and I could clean the wound. As I held the water and vinegar cloth to the wound, Henry moaned loudly. His mother, Mary, began the keening again, and his father took her to the other room, where she could not disturb me and her bleeding son.

"Please, Lydia, do not hurt me any more with that vinegary smelling stuff."

"But I must clean your wound, Henry, or it will fester and be worse."

"Bind it up and let me walk. If I move, that will keep the wound clean."

"No it won't, Henry. You need to keep your leg propped up on the chair and hold it still to heal. Walk later."

"Lydia, I MUST walk now!"

It fast became a losing battle for me, and soon Henry's mother joined in loudly with orders that I must leave Henry alone and let him take care of himself. By this time, Simeon needed my attention and some feeding, so I retreated to the other room where Mary's keening was not as loud and I could have a little space to nurse Sim. As I fed Sim and the people began to leave the house, I thought about the problem of healing Henry. His mother seemed to be determined that he should have his own way, and maybe I should back away from trying to make sense of it all. But, if he would not leave his leg quiet and still to heal, I was certain that it would not heal well, if at all.

One of the local men who had heard of Henry's wound came to see him. He had some advice. His name was Josiah Miles, and Henry said he was an old Indian fighter. He advised Henry to seek a certain Indian Tribe north of us in Pigwacket country, where there was a famous medicine woman named Molly Orcutt who, Capt. Miles said, could cure Henry.

I knew that I could cure Henry, if he would listen to me and not to his mother. The little house was crowded; Henry's mother was still distraught and unreasonable; he was not going to heal in this situation. Reluctantly, as the days—2 or 3 I'm not sure how many—passed, I began to encourage Henry to seek the Indian woman named Molly. Again, he left Simeon and me without money, without our knowing when we would see him again, and I heard him mumble as he limped slowly out the door, "A pox on you all!"

Gradually, life in the little tailoring shop began to settle down to a routine. Mary, Henry's mother, who seemed to rule the household, allowed me to assume the cooking tasks for the family. They were very familiar to me and easy for me to do. Henry's father, who urged me to call him "Pa," was grateful for any thing I did, and he began to teach me to do things that helped him in his business.

Once again, as it had at the Salt Marsh Farm, living beside the ocean became a strong influence on daily life. Whenever the weather was going to change, we had a "seaturn." The smell of the salt foam was evident, as the air moved from over the water onto the land, and people became more high-strung. Simeon would be fractious and hard to please with food, or drink, or amusements like songs or dittys. When the full moon was out, the high tides were very plain to hear. I taught Sim to listen to the sounds, to smell the salty smells, and to love, I hoped, the seaside where we lived.

One of the things I enjoyed learning when we lived at the Tufts cottage was making flax into linen thread. Growing the flax reminded me of my childhood "Salt Marsh Farm." My dear Aunt Deb had taught me her way of dealing with the job, but Pa Tufts knew much more about it than Aunt Deb. When the flax was ripe, which Pa taught me to recognize, we cut it with a scythe and bundled it into "shocks." Those shocks were stored in the barn to dry further. When the stalks that had been wrapped into shocks were very dry, we took the bundles to the Village Flax Pond, undid the shocks, that had been bound together with stalks of the flax, and spread the flax stalks on top of the water. We kept a careful count of the number of the shocks we soaked, as others from the Village of Lee were doing the same thing. The Flax Pond was for everyone to use, on the honor system, and it was in the Village center.

In the late fall we tested the flax, and if the stalks which had by then sunk to the bottom of the pond, were soft enough, we raked them from the pond and "retted" them. For retting, we used a "hatchel," which for the rest of the year became a door stop. The hatchel was a big piece of a log, about a foot square and a foot deep. It was very heavy. Embedded in the log were twelve inch long sharpened spikes that were placed about an inch apart in the wood. It looked like a torture weapon, and was a tool that Simeon was not to go near. Pa taught me to take a few stalks of flax and spread them on the top of the spikes, then, grasping each end of the stalks, to push them down onto and through the spikes, pulling them back and forth until the outer, tough husks fell away in small pieces. This, done over and over, left the soft inner parts of the flax stalk to be twisted into thread with the spinning wheel. It was hard work, and I did it for many days. However, Pa was careful to let me do other things so that my arms and shoulders would not get too achy.

The next step was more fun. I enjoyed the dying process, both for linen and for wool. Sometimes we dyed the flax and the wool before spinning it, and sometimes we dyed it after it was spun into thread or yarn and made into skeins of 40 or 50 yards in length. Those skeins were made with a "niddy-noddy," a hand tool that involved holding a 36 inch long stick with short rods on both ends that would hold the thread or yarn. One complete revolution of the niddy-noddy would make a one yard circle of yarn or thread. By twisting the rod in one hand and stringing the yarn or thread with the other, we counted to 40 or 50, and that made a skein.

Pa taught me to use another kind of winder, which was named a "Weasel." When Simeon was old enough to help us in the weaving room, he would turn the wooden handle, which turned the hand-carved wooden gear and that made the tall spindles go round. One complete turn of the gear made a yard of thread or yarn on the spindles. A peg mounted on the gear was about an inch high. The frame for the whole thing was set on a board that had four legs like a spinning wheel, to which the clapper was attached so that it thwacked loudly with each yard—only the thwacks needed to be counted with the weasel, and it was easier on my arms than the niddy-noddy.

When Sim was turning the handle to help us, I always sang a ditty to him that went something like:
"All around the mulberry bush
The monkey chased the weasel.
Da-da, da-da, da-da-da-da,
POP went the weasel!"
That made the thwacks less scary for Sim, and it also helped him learn to count when the time came for his knowing how to count.

The easiest color to dye was tan. To make it, we picked Goldenrod flowers in the fall, hung them to dry above the fireplace, and in the cold months we used the dried blossoms to add to cold water over the fire, and heat to a boil. Then the linen or wool was soaked in the boiling colored water. When the flax or wool had soaked for two or three hours, or as long as we thought it should, we would remove it from the dying liquid and put it into the mordant, or dye stopper/setter, which we made from vinegar mixed with salt in another, unheated, iron pot that was then heated over the fire. Other people used different native plants to dye, but we usually used Goldenrod flowers because they were all around us in late August and September, easy to pick, and to hang upside down to dry. After the linen or wool was the shade we wanted, we hung the skeins on a rope to dry. We used either a clothesline outside or we strung a rope from the ceiling inside near the fireplace. "Pa" Tufts preferred to dye before the cloth was woven, and so that is the way we did it.

Next came weaving on the very big loom, which was called a "Barn Loom." The loom used about half of the space in the tailoring room. It was as high as the ceiling, and included a bench for the weaver to sit on as well as space to weave 36" wide cloth. It was made of hand hewn beams about four inches thick, and it still showed the adz marks that had shaped the beams, When it was new, it had been painted dark red with "Buttermilk paint." Now, it was so old that it was nearly black in color. All of the corners in the frame had light colored wedges made of oak to hold them firm in place. That loom was very heavy, firm, and sturdy. It also could be taken apart easily.

There were many small things to learn in weaving, and it took me a while to learn to weave anywhere near as well as Pa. We worked together to dress the loom—that is, to take the long hand-spun threads from skeins and put them onto the back of the loom and through the heddles. Those were called the warp threads. When the warp threads were tightened, the weft threads could be wound onto bobbins, inserted into spindles, and then slid through the warp threads to make a solid fabric. We used our feet on pedals to make a space between the warp threads for the shuttle to pass through.

Imported fabrics from England, for the most part, included fancy weaves, such as satins and jacquards, but we made plain fabrics of straight crossed threads, meant to be used for hard, daily, wear. One of the things that took me the longest to learn was how to use the "beater." After the shuttle containing the weft thread had been put through the warp, the beater had to be pulled toward the weaver in a way that was right for the type of fabric to be made. For the jackets and breeches, we made a dense wool fabric that had to have the yarns firmly beaten together. The linsey-woolsey shirt fabric needed a lighter touch on the beater so that the threads were crossed evenly, but not densely.

Finally, one day Pa said, "I think you've got it, Girl, and now you can make the fabric for the shirts the Continentals wear."

I was very proud to hear that. It became my specialty to make the linsey-woolsey into tan checkered material that was thinner and lighter weight than the wool for breeches and jackets. Because the linen thread took the color of the dye differently than the wool yarn, when I varied the number of linen and wool strands in the weft or the warp, the different kinds of checked fabrics pleased both Pa and me.

When the fabrics were woven, we took the pieces off the loom and sent them to the fulling mill in Exeter. There, they were washed, shrunk, dried, and pressed together once more to make the final fabrics that would be sewn.

Cutting and sewing the finished fabrics were the final steps. I remembered my dear Aunt Deb when Pa began to teach me about completing the uniforms. Sewing the uniforms was quite different from sewing my pretty frocks to go to "Bees." Pa had patterns of many sizes for the uniforms, and when we had measured the men who came to order a uniform, we chose the pattern most likely to fit each man. When they returned for a final fitting, they were usually pleased with the results of our labors. After they had tried on the outfits, they paid us 18 English pounds for each uniform.

In the Tailor shop there was space for the customers to be measured for fitting, as well as some chairs for them to wait in. The other downstairs room in the house was the kitchen-dining-living room, a private place for family living. Upstairs were two bedrooms with slanted ceilings and a window at each end of the house. There was only one fireplace upstairs, and two large ones downstairs.

Long before I had learned much about tailoring from Pa Tufts, I had learned a lot about Mary Tufts. Her moods changed minute by minute. She made no secret of the fact that she did not like either me or Simeon, who she insisted, was not her Henry's child, because he looked so much like me. Soon, I was keeping Simeon as much out of her sight as possible, because I thought she might hurt him in some way.

There was no word of my Henry, even from Capt. Miles, and so it seemed best for me to make the most of our situation as it was. When neighbors came to call, Mary would call me "Lie-ja," and tell the visitors that I lied my way into the family by telling Henry that I carried his child, so he, always honorable, had to marry me. She would point out that Simeon did not look at all like Henry, and obviously was no relation to him or any other Tufts.

Pa would often say, "Please, Mary, don't speak about Lydia and Sim like that." She learned to make her attacks when he was not around; Sim and I spent more and more time with Pa, who was always kind and pleasant to us. When he gave advice, it was always quietly, and when he disciplined Sim, it was always with a gentle reminder.

Before we knew it, 1774 was turning into 1775. The calls for uniforms were increasing; "The Sons of Liberty" were now "The Minute Men." By working long hours, we were able to have a variety of sizes of uniforms ready for the men to try, and usually we could fit a man from the rack of already-made uniforms. In January of 1775, Simeon Tufts was just past four years old.

Chapter 5

1775 – 1776

Pa and I were working as fast as we could to make uniforms for the new Continental Army. New uniforms were being ordered faster than we could spin, weave, dye, cut and sew them. Pa talked with me about what we should do to have enough fabric to cut and sew the uniforms. We decided together to buy cloth from the fulling mill that he had used for many years to finish his hand-woven cloth. Pa was able to make a good deal for us with Mr. Tom, the Fuller. Pa was a good and patient teacher, and he helped me to see the importance of being open to new ideas in making decisions that would affect the future for him, for me, and for my Simeon. We thought we were earning good money at 18 Pounds per uniform; we were glad to be busy and to feel successful; we wanted to keep the business growing the way it was.

Mary Tufts continued to lament Henry's fast departure and to blame me for ". . . hounding him out the door on his sore leg." I had long ago learned to ignore her comments, considering the source from whence they came. Because, as Pa said, once Mary made up her mind to hate someone, nothing and nobody would change her mind. Pa also told me a lot about himself, and especially Mary during Henry's young years as we worked at making uniforms.

Pa Tufts had been the younger son in his family. His older brother, Thomas, had inherited enough money for his education at Harvard College in Massachusetts and he became a minister. When Henry came into his teen years, there was no money for his education, so he was apprenticed to a well-known Tailor in Boston, where he earned his keep and a trade, too. Pa seemed to think that was as things should be. He told me that he often wished he had more education, but he did not complain, and he spoke highly of his parents and the trade they had made possible for him to learn. As soon as he had completed his training as a Tailor, he came north to settle in New Hampshire. He and Mary Wedgwood, whom he said was a beautiful girl, were married in 1742 and began to have children. Thomas was their first born. Next was Eliphlet, who served honorably in the Revolution. Their third child, a girl, did not live long enough to be Christened, although Mary always referred to her as "Molly." Their last child was my husband, Henry, born in 1748.

Pa told me, "Mary never completely recovered from the death of our only girl child. She began to lose friends with her unreasonable talk, and soon the name of 'Old Witch Woman' was used by everyone behind her back. After Henry was born, she coddled and fussed over him all the time. As he grew into mischievous boyhood, she never allowed him to be disciplined. She always found a 'reasonable' excuse for any of his misdeeds, whether they were large or small. She encouraged him to do as he pleased, no matter what I, his father, said or did to try to teach him some discipline. So, unbridled and undisciplined, Henry never learned right from wrong."

"I lost all patience with Henry long before he reached the age of twenty. Whenever I tried to explain the ways of the world to him, he not only paid no attention, he laughed at me and did just as he pleased. He began to steal little things like vegetable crops, grain, and a chicken now and then from the neighbors. No amount of talk about how that was wrong made any difference. Henry would just laugh and talk his way out of anything he had done wrong, with his mother's help and occasionally with her money to pay off any serious complainers. His mother tried to teach him to read, write, and to do simple arithmetic. He did well at learning until he decided that he knew enough to make his way in life, and then Mary gave up trying to teach him anything more."

Pa explained how Henry scoffed at the laws of the land. When he asked his father for his "inheritance" to go on a trip into the northern mountains, his father explained that there would be no inheritance for Henry, who was the youngest child in the family. There was no other way for it. If Henry wanted money to go on a journey, he needed to earn it honestly. His father offered to help him find someone in Lee or surrounding Towns who would pay him to work. Shortly thereafter, Henry stole his father's horse and wagon right out of the barn and drove away to parts unknown. In a few weeks, Henry was back, without horse or wagon, and in need of money. When his father questioned him about his deeds, Henry answered, "All I did was to secure my due inheritance. I have no interest in what you call 'Primogeniture Laws!'"

Mary would not discuss the issue with her husband, and so after that Pa said he tolerated, just barely, Henry's presence in the Tufts' home as long as his son was not there very often—just now and then for a very short time. Pa refused to give Henry money no matter what his "need," and Pa guarded his cash very carefully. He strongly urged me to do the same, and never, never, to tell Henry how much I earned from work with Pa.

The warnings that my Bickford relatives, especially my dear Aunt Deb, had tried to give me became clear. When I thought long and hard about these things, I recalled my father's advice so long ago. I had always looked at things "straight," and so I vowed to straighten up my back, use my head, and BE somebody!

As the War loomed closer, more men came to be fitted for uniforms, and so did some snippets of news about my Henry come from near and far. The news of Henry was varied: he was here; he was there; he limped; he didn't limp; he was in jail in at least six places; he had escaped from yet another jail; he had a new "wife;" he had been caught stealing this, and that, and other things. I had learned to listen to those stories, knowing that only some of them could be near the truth. Finally, one day in September of 1775, after the Battles of Lexington and Concord were no longer the latest news, Henry did come.

My heart did flip-flops from the joy of it all when I recognized the angle of his hat and the slight hesitation in his stride as he walked up the road. His mother was ecstatic and wept with joy. Simeon did not recognize him, and clung to my skirts in fear of the tall, dark, man who called him "Son Sim." Pa smiled his one-sided smile, but his eyes did not twinkle. Henry ignored his mother and came straight to me with his smiling eyes and open arms.

"Oh, my Cerulean Beauty, you are SO wise!! Molly Orcott, the Medicine Woman who healed my leg, agreed with your treatment completely. I should have listened to you and stayed here!! When will I ever learn? She did not allow me to walk for months, and when I got somewhat obstreperous, she had her men tie me down in her teepee.

"Unfortunately, I had to repay the Indians 'in kind,' for my care and cure, and so I had to stay with them for the three years to hunt and fish and travel their routes. However, I learned much from them about their ways. I can now be called a Medicine Man, and I can use dyes in ways that you have never heard of, I promise."

It was no surprise and only a slight disappointment to me that Henry had no money for us, but since the talks with Pa, I really had not expected any. I carefully kept my small savings hidden where my husband could not find them, and I watched Henry's subtle ways as he inspected the little house for anything that resembled money or salable items. It was a sobering disappointment, but I had listened carefully to Pa, and to his wise advice. It was a surprise and a relief to me that Henry was ignoring his mother as much as he did during the visit. He was not impolite to her, but he was much more distant in his dealings with Mary than I had observed heretofore. When it was time to retire, Henry went to the small room where Simeon and I slept on the second floor of the little cottage. Our personal reunion was a joy to my lonely heart.

The next day, Henry announced that he would soon be volunteering for service in the Continental Army, and he would appreciate being fitted for a proper uniform. I waited for Pa's reaction to my Henry, and when Pa nodded his gray head, I measured Henry and told him it would be a few weeks before the uniform could be finished.

On the third day after his unannounced arrival, Henry left the little cottage, without saying where he was going or when he would return. I was not surprised. If his mother gave him money, I did not know it, but I thought Mary probably did. I found it hard to do, but I followed Pa's advice and did not give Henry any money when he asked, only a fond farewell. Simeon would smile at his father by the time Henry was taking leave of us, and he waved goodbye with his little four year old hand. It was September, 1775.

I missed my courses in October; I did not wonder at that. I knew that I was very fertile, and that Henry had been very ardent, too. I counted the months, and anticipated a June baby this time.

Henry came home again early in November. He had resolved, he told us, to enlist for two months at the next opportunity, or whenever his uniform was ready. On November fifth, with his uniform on his arm, Henry took the Oath to serve and became a Private in Capt. Smith Emerson's Company for 2 months duration. He would receive a good bonus for his service, and I was hopeful that he would bring some of it home with him.

The next time we saw my husband was in February, 1776. He was quick to apologize for his lack of money for Simeon and me, but he had lost all of his bonus money from serving in Portsmouth Harbor by betting on a wrestling match, he said. He was interested in making enough money to support us, and he would do so in the future with his wrestling skills as they improved, he assured me. During the next several months, I mended his broken left wrist and his dislocated right elbow as well as other minor injuries—all from wrestling—without receiving any earnings from Henry's bouts that had caused the injuries, or from the money for his service in the Continental Army.

Pa had noticed my family condition, and in his usual kind way, he had brought up the subject by inquiring whether Henry and I expected to increase our family. I told him about the June baby that was due, and he smiled encouragement and understanding. He said,

"Well, we'll make out all right. We'll have some uniforms made up ahead, and I'll hire a woman to look after Mary so that you can have as peaceful a time as possible."

Mary did not notice my growing belly, and I did not mention it to her, for fear of exciting her for no reason. She was easily excited, especially by anything I said these days, so I stayed carefully away from her most of the time.

Simeon was increasing in years and in knowledge, and his idea of my growing size was happiness that he would maybe have a little brother to play with. He was counting well, and kept count of the months left until June and new baby's arrival time.

Pa made a "chapbook" for Sim to use with his reading lessons, and we practiced a little each day with Bible verses, the alphabet, and syllables for sounding out strange new words. The Chapbook hung on a hook low on the wall of the tailoring room, and whenever Sim needed something to do, he took it down and looked at it. It was a thin board with paper glued onto one side. On the paper Pa and I together had printed words from the Bible, the alphabet letters, and the syllables for Sim to practice. Whenever he had mastered one paper, we made another and glued it on top of the mastered work. Ciphering, or arithmetic, was part of our everyday life in the tailor shop, and so both Pa and I included Simeon in working with yardages, threads-per-inch, and so forth. Sim learned about money quickly, and soon he was able to make change as men paid for their uniforms. Pa and I were proud of him as the months passed.

Henry learned of the new baby during the spring of 1776. It was about the time of his signing, along with his brother, Thomas, and his father, Henry Sr., of the Association Test of Lee, N.H. All those who signed the Test promised to oppose the British at the risk of their own lives and fortunes. The Revolutionary War, as it was now called, was heating up and Henry had re-enlisted for two month periods twice more. He told me that he was pleased about a new baby, but he did not change his habit of staying with me and Simeon for very short visits whenever he happened to be in Lee.

As June approached, Pa and I made plans and extra uniforms for the weeks I would be confined. My term thus far had gone well, and I was feeling as well as when I carried Simeon. Could it be another boy? If so, I thought about names for him. I talked with Pa, and he allowed that each generation of the Tufts family had a Thomas. It was decided then, that if the baby were a boy, he would be named Thomas.

When my labor came, it was short, and a healthy baby boy was born in the little tailoring cottage. The mid-wife was my friend, and she was a good coach and careful of her work at the delivery. I was pleased, and "Baby Thomas" was strong, healthy, and suckled like a good one right away.

The woman Pa had hired to care for Mary was told that Mary was not to be left alone with me or either of my boys, and she said that she understood. Mary was not able to talk sensibly any more those days, and she did not seem to understand when anyone spoke to her. She was in her own world, Pa said, and he grieved for her. I grieved for him, because it was plain to me that he still loved her. I knew that was possible, because I still felt the thrill in my heart every time I saw my Henry coming home to us and every time he smiled at me in his eyes and called me his silly pet name, "Cerulean Beauty."

One day during my confinement, Pa went to the fulling mill for an order of cloth for uniforms. He came home shakng his head. My Henry had been caught hiding cloth in Pa's barn that he and Ezekial Hubbard had stolen from Tom's fulling mill. Henry was in Exeter Jail, awaiting sentencing for the crime. Pa was especially sad to learn that his barn was the hiding place Henry had chosen. He was wondering if he should end Henry's visits, and I begged him not to do that. I promised to watch my husband constantly while he visited us, and so Pa did not ban Henry from the Tufts home. He did tell me that the neighbors were all up in arms over Henry's activities, especially with the new baby in the house, and the work Pa and I were trying to do. Pa attempted to calm them down, he said, but he wasn't sure that he had succeeded.

During that talk, I had been so interested that I had forgotten to watch Baby Thomas's cradle by the fireplace in my bedroom. Suddenly, we heard a tiny baby scream as if in terrible pain. I looked in the cradle and he was missing. Pa searched all over the second floor and I ran downstairs to search on the first floor. Baby Thomas was screaming in pain as he flailed his arms and legs where he lay naked on the spikes of the hatchel, which sat near the door of the tailoring room. Mary was nowhere to be seen, but it was her work, I knew instantly.

Thomas was bleeding badly as I plucked him off the spikes and began to try to comfort him. I found his blanket on the floor and wrapped him in it to stanch the flow of blood. As soon as I could get cool water mixed with vinegar, I bathed his back, head, arms, and legs to ebb the flow of blood. The vinegar soon cleaned him up, and although I ached with pity that the vinegar water mixture hurt him, it cleansed his wounds, which were not deep, but were about an inch apart over the back side of his entire head and body.

Chapter 6

1776

Simeon, Baby Thomas, and I were in the small second floor room we shared in the little tailoring cottage in Lee. Baby Thomas was quieted down a little from his ordeal on the hatchel, and he seemed about to drop off to sleep as he suckled. There was a tap on the door.

"Come in."

"Lydia, it's Pa. I'm so very sorry about what happened to Baby Thomas, I don't know how to tell you how sorry I am. We need to talk and make some plans for us all. I hope the bleeding has stopped, and that he is okay."

"He's nearly asleep, now, Pa, and of course nothing that happened to him is your fault. I agree we need to make some plans so that something worse does not happen to him. Have you talked to Mary? Do you know why she did such a thing?"

"She told me that she thinks Baby Thomas is really Baby Henry, and she was taking care of him when she heard someone coming, and so she put him down on the nearest thing she could see. It happened to be the hatchel. I believe her, Lydia, I think she is not able to think any further into things than that. However, no one can say that she will not do something else as dangerous to him. I have also talked to Sadie, who left Mary alone long enough for this to happen. She will be leaving as soon as I can find someone else to watch over Mary."

"Do you have any ideas about what we can do in the future to be sure Baby Thomas is safe? I am nearly ready to come back to work in the Tailoring Shop, but I cannot be away from him with Mary watching for her chance to pick him up."

"I have sent for my son Thomas up in Northwood. He will have some ideas, I think. He knows how his mother is, and he will understand our problem. I also have some other news that you need to know."

The back of my neck began to tingle. 'Other news' said in that way by Pa could only mean news of my Henry.

"The neighbors are up in arms over Henry's actions, in light of another baby in the family, our work, Mary as she is, and all that we are trying to do, plus all the stealing he has done. He was in Exeter Jail for stealing the cloth from Fuller Tom, but he escaped, and is headed this way, they think. They want to lynch him, Lydia. I know he doesn't act right, but I can't be a party to killing my own son! We must do something to help save his life."

The back of my neck began to shiver with this news. Speechless, I could only nod my head in agreement. Carefully, so as not to wake him, I put Baby Thomas into his cradle, on a soft bed of cotton wool. He cried out briefly as I laid him on his back, but he soon settled into sleep again.

"We can hide Henry for a little while, but we cannot keep him here for a long time. He's sure to get restless and do something so that he'd be found out, and we'd be in trouble for harboring him."

"How soon can Thomas get here?"

"If he starts out as soon as he gets my message, he could be here by tomorrow afternoon. We need to think about how we can plan with him. If you will think, I will too, Lydia, and we'll all come up with something."

After Pa left, I talked with Simeon. It was the summer of 1776, and the little boy was only five years old. He needed to have his questions answered and the grown-up matters needed to be made clear to him.

"Sim, do you understand what Pa and I were talking about?"

"I think so, Mama. Gram Mary did something dangerous to Baby Thomas, and Uncle Tom is coming down to help you and my Pa figure out what can be done. Baby Thomas is not safe here, I know. I love him, Ma, I want him to grow big enough to play with me."

"That's right, Sim. Now, maybe you can help me think of a plan we can make to be sure Baby Thomas is safe when you and I go back to work in the Tailor Shop with Pa. Will you share your thoughts with me? Let's close our eyes and think for awhile."

As I had hoped, Simeon soon dropped off to sleep, and I was able to do some serious thinking. Facts crowded my head: First, Mary Tufts is truly the "Old Witch Woman" that the neighbors call her. She is not responsible for her actions, and she will surely harm dear Baby Thomas if something is not done; Second, Pa needs me to get back to work making uniforms as soon as I am strong enough; Third, Henry's life is in danger from his own actions, but he must be helped; Fourth, Pa has saved my life and Simeon's, and we need to help him do whatever he and Brother Thomas decide to do about the situation.

"There, now, Lydia," I told myself, "It's time you remembered your father's advice once more. 'Stand up straight and tall, hold up your head, and BE somebody.'" I was also reminded of my dear Aunt Deborah, who was kind to me and patient when I made mistakes. Strangely, that eased my mind, too.

After a short nap, Sim and I took Baby Thomas downstairs and got some supper on the table. Pa was able to eat a little, but he was very quiet and thoughtful. Sadie was very attentive to Mary, and very anxious to please Pa and me. She felt badly about Mary's deeds, I knew. However, facts were facts, she did not do as she had been told, and so she would be leaving as soon as Pa found someone else to look after Mary. That was the way people like Mary who were not right in their minds were taken care of in those days. She had been a young teenager when they were married, Pa told me, and she did not adjust to marriage, having children, and then a dead baby in such a short time. Pa put out the word that he needed help, and soon someone would come to his rescue, he knew and I trusted.

The baby was less fretful, and more comfortable with the Aloe that I had been putting on his wounds after I cleaned them with the vinegar water. The wounds were not deep, and when they formed scabs, I knew his skin would heal under the scabs. My worry began to shift from Thomas to keeping Mary away from him so that he could heal safely.

That night was a sleepless one. As soon as Sadie was asleep and Pa was dozing in his chair downstairs, Mary's footsteps creaked the floorboards in the room next to ours. I had braced a chair against the door to our bedroom, but I heard the doorlatch jiggle, and I knew that Mary was prowling. Before Baby Thomas was born, I had not worried about Mary's night wanderings, because I knew that she was afraid of me, and her fear seemed to overcome her hatred of me and Simeon. However, her certainty that Baby Thomas was really her baby Henry was unshakeable. No one could convince her that the baby was Henry's son and not Henry. It was a matter that I knew I could not do anything about, so I left it. However, I needed to be aware of Mary's night wanderings and keep my baby safe.

Next day, the time for Brother Thomas to arrive seemed to pass very slowly. Simeon and I practiced his reading, his writing, and he added, subtracted, and then did all those things over again. I did not dare to leave the baby, so

Simeon did not get to play out of doors that day. He was delighted when Pa invited him to help with weaving for a while, and he went downstairs to sit at the loom with his Grandpa.

Between feeding and caring for Baby Thomas's wounds, I got our noon meal and then put I some soup on the fire to have for our evening meal. Brother Thomas might like some when he arrived later that afternoon, and I made some blueberry biscuits to go with the soup for our supper. The biscuits rose in the oven as they baked, and they did not need a long time to cook. Sadie quietly distracted Mary, and she did not try to touch the baby during that day. Her sad eyes as she looked into the cradle made me uncomfortable, but we all watched her carefully, and her hands were prevented from touching him by one of us who was always nearby.

Pa received a message from Henry that day, too. There was always a way, Henry had found, to get word to his father when he needed something. This time, Pa told me, he sent word to Henry to stay away and await further word from home. Pa did not refuse help, but was careful that any help he gave Henry would not endanger me or my children.

A little after darkness, Thomas tapped on the door of the tailoring room. He was tall and dark, like my Henry, but his eyes did not smile often. He was quiet, not a talker, and was very serious about things. He had left his new young wife on their farm in Northwood, where he was homesteading one hundred upland acres for a home for them and their many hoped-for children, so he said. No one in Lee had met his young wife, but he told us her name was Elizabeth, that she was seventeen, very pretty, could cook and sew, spin, and weave, 'with the best of 'em.' He seemed very happy and proud of his life situation. He spoke respectfully to his mother, and did not ask what had happened to bandaged Baby Thomas until after we had eaten and Mary had gone upstairs with Sadie.

Pa began our story, and he told it well, I thought. Thomas shook his head in sympathy.

When Pa said, "We need to come up with a plan that will make sure that Baby Thomas is safe and can grow up well. We also need to help Henry out of his present mess and save his life. Lydia and I also need to get back to work making uniforms—we are behind with our orders, Lydia and I tried to get some uniforms made ahead so that she could get well from the birthing of the baby in peace, but here we are."

Thomas replied, "Let me think on all of this, and tomorrow, after I have a good sleep, I will try to have an idea for you to think about. Meanwhile, Simeon, I would like to talk with you a little bit. Tell me, do you read?"

"Yes, sir."

"Would you show me?"

"Yes, Sir."

Like Thomas, Simeon did not use any extra words. He read from his chapbook, and Thomas praised him. Simeon showed his uncle how he could write, and how he could add and subtract. His uncle seemed to think my Sim did well.

"You've done a good job, Lydia."

"Thank you, Thomas, Simeon has been a good pupil. He seems to like to learn." Thomas looked straight at me and said, "Do you intend to stay here with my father and my mother in the future?" I answered, "Your father saved my life when I came to him with Simeon and in desperation. I can never forget that. He has taught me how to make a living for myself and Simeon, and he has put Mary's craziness and Henry's, too, in terms that make sense, and that I can understand and accept, as he has done. I can not leave him after he has treated me so well, and I am just beginning to be able to pay him back a little bit with my work in the Tailoring Shop."

At that, Pa smiled a broad smile, and I stopped talking. That night was a repeat of the night before. As soon as everyone had settled down for the night, the door latch to the room where Sim and Thomas and I were to sleep rattled. I had placed the chair to brace the door closed. However, this time the door opened wide enough for Mary's hand to get through it and to push the chair aside. I sat up in bed, and said,

"Mary, don't come in here and don't touch Baby Thomas!"

"Liedja, you know that is my baby Henry, and you know that you have stolen him from me. I'm going to get you, and you know that, too. I'll kill you if I can!"

Chapter 7

To Northwood
1776

The next morning found me groggy from lack of sleep and as frightened as I had ever been for both my children and myself. It had been very hard to get Mary back into her own room with Sadie, and to quiet down. Sim and Baby Thomas were roused, too, and Brother Thomas and Pa were upstairs in a flash when they heard Mary shouting. Sadie, Pa, and Thomas restrained Mary and got her into her own bed. Then Pa and Brother Thomas showed me how to put a chair back under the door latch to make a kind of lock for it, and then we all tried to go back to sleep.

Pa and Thomas had talked during the night, and they shared their ideas. It had been decided that my boys and I, Henry, and Brother Thomas were to go to Northwood as soon as we could get ready. Even though I had given birth much too recently to do it, I knew that I must find the courage to travel the eighteen or so miles to Northwood today by horse and wagon.

Pa sent word to Henry to meet us in Nottingham, which was far enough away from Lee and the other towns where Henry had robbed farmers, that he should be safe from lynching even if he showed his face. Pa would loan us his Buckboard wagon that he used to carry cloth to and from the Fulling Mill and "Kit," his trusty old mare, for me to drive back to Lee later. The back of the wagon was filled with hay for Kit, since Thomas's first crop was not yet mowed down and would not be dry enough to use for feed during the time we would be in Northwood. The hay also made a good place for Baby Thomas's cradle to travel, and Simeon could nap there when he got tired.

Simeon was very excited. He was about to go on his first long journey by horse and wagon! Thomas told me it would all work out, he thought, and we would talk about some ideas he and Pa had spoken of when they talked the night before.

We packed a meal to eat on the way as well as a change of clothes for Sim and me and some aloe and vinegar water for Baby Thomas's wounds. Before noontime, we set off from Lee for Northwood, planning to travel twelve to fourteen hours and a distance of about eighteen miles. I sat on a pillow to keep me as comfortable as possible, because the bench and the wagon had no springs. I was determined to do it, and so I straightened up my backbone, and got onto that wagon. I was getting my courage up and ready to BE somebody.

Sim settled into the hay in the back of the wagon, and we placed Thomas's cradle just behind the seat where Brother Thomas and I sat so that I could reach it when the baby needed attention. Kit arched her old neck, and looked as if she was pleased to be pulling us in the old wagon. Sim enjoyed the hay, I could see, and waved his hand to everyone we saw on the road.

After we were out of sight of the Tufts cottage, Thomas cleared his throat, and I knew he was ready to talk a little.

"I am anxious, Thomas, to hear what you and Pa talked of as ideas about what we can do about Mary and the Baby. I believe that Pa will find someone who can understand her better than Sadie does, and so what happened last night and before won't happen again."

"I think you're right, Lydia, but Mother Mary will have to stay in the cottage in Lee. There is no other way for her to be taken care of. She may get worse, and have to be restrained more, if she goes totally out of her mind, and I think you should be ready to face that. She seems to leave Simeon alone, and he is wise enough to stay away from her. I have watched carefully, and she does not seem to threaten him in any way. However, she will probably never leave Thomas alone. She is convinced that he is Henry come back to her. Did she ever threaten you before last night?"

"No, Thomas, she never threatened me before. Her favorite name for me has been 'Liedja', because she wants people to know that she thinks I lied about Simeon being Henry's child, and as proof, she thinks Sim does not in any way look like Henry. I just pretend that I don't hear her when she talks like that, and I've told Sim not to hear it, either. Pa cannot reason with her, and it is so plain that he loves her still, I don't like to make trouble over it, so I don't talk about it, or even think about it much.

"You are an unusual person, Lydia. It must hurt when Mother Mary is so rotten to you."

"It does hurt, Thomas, but Pa has been so kind to me and to Simeon, I have come to be very fond of him. My father died twenty two years ago when I was twelve, and Pa has taken his place, I should say, very well. I also think that Mary is sick, at least in the head, or she wouldn't say and do the bad things she does. I don't know what to do to protect Baby Thomas until he is old enough to look after himself with her, but I hope that we can come up with something."

"Well, Lydia, I hope that we can. I want to talk with Elizabeth when we get home, and maybe she and I can think of something to help you. Pa says he doesn't know what he would do without you to keep the house and the business going. You were sent by God he believes, to take care of things in Lee. What would you do if you didn't stay with Pa in Lee?"

"I have no where else to go, Thomas. My Bickford relatives have made it plain that they have no room for me, in spite of their need for some help with sicknesses and birthings now and then, they do not have the room for me and my children in either their homes or their hearts, and they do not want my Henry around any of their places."

"I see, Lydia. Henry is a major problem for you, then. Pa has always said that if Mary had allowed some discipline into Henry's young life, he might know right from wrong by now. What do you think?"

"I think that Pa is right. Without some training while we are young, most of us would grow up not knowing right from wrong. But, Thomas, I love Henry. I have been in love with him ever since I first saw him at a Husking Bee years ago. I cannot help myself. I know that he doesn't do right by me and by Simeon and Baby Thomas, and I doubt he ever will. However, I love him, that's all there is to it! Seeing Pa's love for Mary in spite of her ways has proven to me that it is possible to love someone nobody else can stand."

"That is clear to see, Lydia, and speaking of the Devil himself, there's Henry now—on his way to Nottingham, I daresay."

There was my Henry, with his hat at the special angle and the hesitation in his stride.

Thomas pulled up on the reins, and Henry climbed into the back of the wagon. He was not very talkative, and quickly buried himself in the hay. As we moved on again, Thomas and Henry talked enough for me to learn that Henry had a bad scare on the road to Nottingham, and he was very happy to see us coming along. He peeked at the baby, and smiled the smile that always stole my heart.

"My son, my son. Will you be a Cerulean Lad like your older brother? I hope that you will be a copy of me—not in actions, but in looks."

"Your mother has taken it into her head that Baby Thomas is really you, my brother, and she has seriously threatened Lydia's life. We are on our way to see my wife Elizabeth and talk about what can be done about the things going on in the house in Lee."

"I thought Father had hired a woman to keep Mother under control."

Thomas replied, "It didn't work well. The girl let Mother get away from her, and our Mother nearly killed the baby."

"However could she do that?"

"She thought she would care for his needs she told me, she got startled and put him down, not too gently, on the spikes of the hatchel in the Tailoring Room. Lydia has done all she can to heal his wounds, but it will take time for them to heal—there are many on his back and head as well as his arms and legs."

By now, Simeon was awake and staring at Henry with his very blue eyes wide. Henry turned to him.

"And how are you, my Cerulean Lad? I hope that your mother is really teaching you to read, and write, and figure, because those things are important to grown-ups, you know."

"Yes, Sir, she is." And that seemed to close the subject. Sim looked into the baby's cradle. "Thomas has his eyes open, Mama, can I play with him now?"

"You can talk to him and lightly touch his hands, Sim, but please do not try to pick him up. It hurts him to be moved."

We would soon be getting close to the southern part of Northwood, Thomas told us, but we needed to cross to the northern part of the town before we came to his holdings. He told

Henry that he owned a thick grove of small fir trees toward the back part of his land. It was high and dry, and Henry was welcome to make himself at home there. The cabin would not hold Thomas and his wife Elizabeth as well as me and my boys, so Henry should hide out in the fir trees. He could come to the cabin to visit his family, but should run into the firs if someone came near.

Henry agreed to those conditions. He had been really frightened by his experience on the road to Nottingham, and he seemed to be grateful for the refuge in his brother's fir trees. The road narrowed as we went along, and soon became wagon tracks with tall grass between them. The high wheels on the Buckboard kept us above the grass and we moved along well.

We had traveled under tall trees for a while, when Thomas again pulled Kit up.

"Now, we are on my land, and I want to bid you welcome. I will call Elizabeth in my usual way."

He put his thumb and forefinger into his lips and blew a loud, piercing whistle, and in a split second we all heard an answering whistle, a bit higher in pitch. Out from the woods bounced a lovely girl, running as fast as a deer. I liked the look of her. She was smiling, with her eyes as well as her mouth, but she stopped suddenly as she saw that Thomas was not alone.

"Come, my Sprite," said Thomas, "I want you to meet my brother, Henry, his wife, Lydia, his son, Simeon, and Baby Thomas, too."

Elizabeth approached our wagon shyly, and greeted each one of us, by shaking our hands in turn. When she got to Henry, she seemed to shrink in size and she dropped her eyes to one side. She did not seem able to look him in the eye. I saw that, but I did not feel any foreboding by it. When she peeked into the cradle, she looked longingly at Baby Thomas, who had dropped back to sleep and was peaceful.

"We have much to tell you, Elizabeth, and we will tell you all about things in Lee as soon as we are settled in the cabin."

To me, he said, "Over there, Lydia, small but room enough for us."

We pulled up to the cabin and Thomas lifted out the cradle with Baby Thomas in it.

"Lydia needs lots of rest," he said to Elizabeth, "She is traveling very soon after the birth. Will you help her?"

Elizabeth took my arm with kindness and carried the pillow in her other hand. As we entered the cabin door, she said,

"Welcome, Sister Lydia. Please be at home with us."

She guided me to the bunk bed, and I gratefully collapsed upon it.

"The baby is beautiful. How old is he? May I pick him up? Someday, I hope to have my own Thomas Tufts, Jr, and I hope that he will be as beautiful as this one. Oh, my, what has happened to him?"

I explained as simply as I could what made Baby Thomas's wounds, and suggested that we talk about it further when the rest of the group was with us. Elizabeth bustled around the fire and we soon had a good meal that had been cooking as we arrived.

After we had eaten and all, including Henry, were still gathered around the table, Thomas said,

"Now it is time we talked. Lydia is devoted to my parents in Lee. She and Pa have a good tailoring business going, and they both want to keep it going. Henry is Henry. Lydia accepts his restlessness, but he does not seem to change his habits now that he has children and parents who are aging and sometimes need help."

Henry got up from his chair, and allowed as how he was very tired and would retire to his fir trees. When he took leave of our hostess, he bowed and kissed her hand. She blushed crimson red, and withdrew her hand quickly from his grasp. He gave me a quick kiss on the cheek. He seemed to forget his sons completely as he went out the door.

Elizabeth hung her head as she watched him go. When she looked up at Thomas, she asked to speak to him alone. I turned my back, and attended to Baby Thomas, who seemed very hungry. Simeon was trying to keep his heavy lidded eyes open, and I suggested that he go up the ladder to the sleeping loft and go to sleep. He was ready to follow that suggestion.

When Elizabeth, Thomas and I were together again, Thomas began.

"Lydia, you will have to understand that Henry makes Elizabeth very nervous. She may be only seventeen, but she is a very grown-up seventeen. She does not want Henry around her, because of his ways. Please forgive her, and understand. She is willing to cook his meals, but I will take them to him. I do not want him in this cabin again. If you want to see him, I'll show you how to find him. I don't expect he'll be content to stay in hiding very long, but he can use the fir grove as long as he wants. Tomorrow, Elizabeth and I will have something more to talk with you about Baby Thomas, but we all need a good night's sleep now. 'Liz and I will go up to the sleeping loft for tonight. Sleep well, Lydia."

My curiosity really had the sleep fairy on the run that night, but I did finally drop off to sleep. When I woke in the dark, my Simeon was beside me. In the morning, he told me that he had trouble settling down in the sleeping loft above. When Sim and I finally opened our eyes, Elizabeth was working around the fire and getting breakfast. Thomas was no where to be seen, and Baby Thomas was still asleep from the last feeding I had given him in the dark hours of night.

Thomas entered the cabin.

"Henry sends his thanks for the food, Elizabeth, and he will rest in the fir trees for a few more hours. If you and Simeon want to see him, Lydia, I will show you how to find him, whenever you are ready to walk a bit."

"Thank you, Thomas, but I think I'll not walk very much for awhile."

"Then, if you are ready to hear it, Elizabeth and I have something to talk with you about."

I did not like the tone of Thomas's voice, it was very serious and sober. "I'm ready."

I rocked Thomas's cradle gently with my foot and put my arm around Simeon as I looked at Thomas and Elizabeth with their somber faces.

"Elizabeth has heard all about the life you face in Lee, and she is so sorry about the baby. We both are grateful to you for your help for Pa and keeping his home and business going with him. We would help if we lived nearer to Lee, but it is not possible for us to have our lives here in Northwood and in Lee, too. Our offer to you is that we will raise Thomas here, and treat him as our own. There are a few things about the way we want to do it that you may not like, but you are strong and will understand why we want it this way, we hope. If we take Thomas to raise as our own, we want to adopt him. Above all, he is not to know that Henry is his father, and he is never to see him as an uncle, either. We also do not want Thomas to know that you are his mother. He must be totally Elizabeth's and mine. Can you accept that?"

Chapter 8

1776

That was the longest speech I had heard from Thomas's lips. He and Elizabeth had certainly talked a lot the night before he said all of that talk. I was not surprised that they wanted to take Baby Thomas for their own. It certainly meant safety for him. However, I had held him close to my heart for so long that I needed to get used to the idea he would no longer be mine. I thought about what the situation was in Lee, and how Mary was sure to behave with Baby Thomas, and that gave me unpleasant pictures to help me with the decision. The things I knew about birthings told me that it would not be easy to interrupt my body's natural production of milk for the baby, but that I could overcome. With bowed head, I said a short prayer for help from the Lord to get me through this time in my life. In my mind, I heard my father say once again,

"Straighten up your spine, Lydia, hold up your head, and BE somebody."

Then, I looked Thomas and Elizabeth straight in the eye, took a deep breath, and said, "I agree."

That was it. We began to plan the changes for Baby Thomas. Elizabeth was to slowly take over the baby's care, and I would help her learn all she needed to know, especially the care of his wounds. Thomas would search for a wet nurse to feed him until he could take cow's milk from a special cup with a spout on it. Simeon and I would remain in Northwood until both Elizabeth and Brother Thomas were comfortable with the care of Baby Thomas.

Suddenly, I remembered Simeon and my Henry. I needed to speak with Simeon to be sure that he understood the whole matter, but Henry's actions the day before had shown me that he was not concerned for either of his sons. He would not miss his second son at all, I thought. Where was Simeon? We called his name again and again. There was no answer. I was torn between staying close to Baby Thomas and running into the woods to search for Sim. Brother Thomas had the same idea at about the same time.

"I'll go to the fir grove, Lydia, to see if Simeon has gone there to look for Henry."

"Thank you, Thomas."

Elizabeth and I sat down to look at Baby Thomas's scars, and they were looking a little better. The Aloe was helping scabs to form, and it was plain to see that healthy skin was beginning to grow underneath the scabs.

"I think that plain soap and water washes will do for his skin, now, Elizabeth, and then some Aloe rubbed gently on over the scabs will make him feel better."

For his sake, I did not put tight clothing onto Baby Thomas, but wrapped him loosely in a blanket. As I looked into his dark eyes, I was startled to feel strongly that this baby would grow into an image of his real father, who looked so much like Brother Thomas that I was sure my decision was the right one.

"Elizabeth, I think this baby will grow to look exactly like his father, who looks so much like your Thomas. His eyes would be turning lighter by now if they were going to change as he grows. I don't think that you have a 'Cerulean Lad' here."

Elizabeth smiled. "It must be so hard for you, Lydia, to think of meeting our terms for taking the baby. I admire your courage."

"It is not easy to carry a babe so close to my heart for all those months and then to give him up so that I will not see him at five years of age, or ten, or any other age, but I'm sure you and Thomas will raise him well and he will be a good man someday. If he should return to Lee with Sim and me, who knows what else might happen to him? Sim and I do not have any other place to go or to live. I'm grateful to both you and Thomas for your kindnesses. Of course, I will miss the baby, but I know he'll be safe, and I think that his staying with you is the best choice we have, Sim, and Thomas, and I."

"Mama, Mama," sang like music to my ears from the door of the cabin. Thomas and Simeon were returning from the woods, where Sim had been looking for his father.

"I'm SO glad to see you, Sim. Were you looking for your father? It's not safe for you to go into the woods alone. I'm sure that you've learned that now. We live in open seashore land, and you're used to that kind of country. These tall trees make it so easy to get lost. Please don't go out of sight of the cabin again, Sim."

"I won't, Mama. Uncle Tom has asked me if I'd like to go with him to town today to try to find a wet nurse. Can I? Can I please? He promised to tell me what a wet nurse is, too."

"You may go, Sim, if you promise me you'll mind your Uncle every time he tells you to do something or not to do something."

"I will, Mama, I will."

"If you promise me, I know you will, son. Now, I would like to talk with you about something else. While you were looking for your father, your Aunt and Uncle and I were talking about how to look out for Baby Thomas's safety. They would like to keep him here with them and help him to grow up here in Northwood."

"I know, Mama, Uncle Tom told me about it as we walked home. I can play with Thomas when he is big enough, but he'll live here and I'll have to come here and see him to play."

"What's this 'Uncle Tom'? You know it's not good manners to use a nickname like 'Tom' unless the person tells you to."

"But he did, Mama, on the way home, he said I should call him 'Uncle Tom.'"

As soon as Thomas could speak with me quietly, he said,

"Lydia, Sim did not find his father, and we came home by way of the fir grove. Henry has left, and he did not leave any sign to tell us what direction he headed. I am so sorry. He should be here to take care of you and Sim as well as his father and mother."

"Thomas, you're kind, but ever since Henry and I were married, 't'was ever thus' is all I can say. I am used to taking care of Sim and me as well as Pa and Mary."

Thomas and Simeon set off with Thomas's horse and small wagon after the breakfast that Elizabeth had cooked. For her young years, she was a good cook. Over the fire, she had made a breakfast "Hotch Potch" of bacon, eggs, oats, and wheat. It was hearty and good tasting with a hot slice of brown bread from the oven. Elizabeth made good butter, and that made the hot bread taste even better.

While Thomas and Simeon were gone, Elizabeth and I took turns rocking Baby Thomas in our arms and in his cradle as we talked and talked. I became very comfortable about her caring for the baby, and I took a restful nap before Thomas and Sim came back.

Thomas had good news. He had found a woman who would come to them and stay until Baby Thomas was able to take cow's milk from the special cup. She would arrive in two days, and then, after everyone was comfortable with the arrangements in the Northwood cabin, Simeon and I would take the Buckboard with old Kit and go back to Lee.

During the remaining days we stayed in Northwood, I rested and gained strength. Sim tagged after his Uncle Tom as though he were Thomas's shadow. I smiled as I noticed a certain style to Sim's young walk that imitated his Uncle's. Elizabeth noticed it too, and we often shared a smile and a wink as we watched the "men" go about their outside work. Elizabeth gradually took on more and more of the care of Baby Thomas. The wet nurse, who was a large, motherly woman of about 35, with a good supply of milk for the baby, was named Triphenia. She asked to be called "Trippy."

When Trippy joined us in the tiny cabin, the sleeping arrangements changed, because Baby Thomas needed night feedings. Sim and I climbed the ladder each night to the sleeping loft. Trippy and Elizabeth shared the big bed on the first floor, and Brother Thomas slept on a cot he had made for the downstairs. Trippy took the night feedings, and I began to sleep all night. The baby's skin began to heal so well that the scabs were dropping off, and he waved his little arms and legs with the joy of a typical new babe. I was happy to see that he was thriving with the care of Liz and Trippy.

When Trippy heard Baby Thomas's story and why he needed her, she wept.

"No tiny baby should enter the world with such a thing happening to him in the first days of his life," she said. "And, you're going back there to live? Why?"

"I have no other family and no other place to go, Trippy, and my husband's father, whom I call Pa, is very good to us. He needs us, both for his tailoring business and to take care of his house for him. He's not getting any younger, and he's so lonely, without his Mary able to be beside him, I feel sorry for him."

When Trippy had taken over most of Baby Thomas' feeding, Simeon noticed that the front of my dress was wet.

"What's that on your dress, Mama? Did you spill something on yourself?"

"No, Thomas, that is the milk that my body makes for Thomas, but he doesn't need it anymore. Trippy is feeding him most of the time, now."

There was no need to tell the little boy about the almost constant ache and the tender lumps in my breasts that were the signs of the process of weaning the baby and drying up my milk production.

"As soon as Trippy is feeding Baby Thomas all of the time, you and I will take Old Kit and the Buckboard wagon and go back to Lee. I think Pa Tufts will be glad to see us. Don't you miss him? I do."

"Yes, I miss my Pa Tufts. I don't miss my Gram Mary, though. I'm afraid of her. She says bad things to us."

"Your Gram Mary is not herself, Sim. She is sick, and we need to remember that. Even though she looks like she always did, she is not the same these days. Remember to be kind to her, but stay near me or Pa all the time, please."

The day came to harness Kit and hitch her to the wagon. All that could be done to make an easy transition into his new family had been done for Baby Thomas. Elizabeth cried a few tears saying, "Thank you," many times, and packed a good meal for us to eat on the road. Sim and I each took Baby Thomas in our arms for a quiet goodbye, and a kiss to his cheek. Then we were on the road to our home.

Sim called to his Aunt and Uncle,

"Goodbye, Aunt 'Liz and Uncle Tom, I'll see you in the Spring!"

The old Buckboard wagon was much lighter than it had been on the trip to Northwood, with no cradle and Baby Thomas, hay, Henry, or Brother Thomas on board. Simeon and I went along to the south at a good pace. When Sim needed to rest, he stretched out behind the seat on the pillow I had used to go to Northwood, and when he was awake and needed something to do, he took the reins and guided Kit for a little while.

While he was awake, he chattered like a Magpie. He told me of all the wonderful things his Uncle Tom had told him.

"When I grow up, I want to be just like Uncle Tom. I want to make my home on land that no one else has ever lived on. I want to cut down trees and plow ground that no one else has ever plowed. Uncle Tom says that is the best way, and new land gives the best crops."

I smiled at Sim's excitement, and I knew that his Uncle Tom was a good model for him to copy.

"If you want to do those things, Sim, there's no one who can stop you. There's still much land to be settled, and I'll be proud of you if you are like your Uncle Tom when you grow up. He's a good man."

While Sim was sleeping, I wondered what we would find in the little Tailor's cottage in Lee. Thomas had sent word to Pa about our plans, and he had sent further word to Pa when our day to travel had been settled on.

By the time we reached Lee and the tailor shop, it would be December of 1776, and Sim would be five years old.

Chapter 9

1776 ~ 1779

The trip south to Lee went well. The lunch that Elizabeth had packed for us tasted good, and soon after Sim had eaten, he was content to lie down on the pillow just in back of the wagon seat and take a nap. Relaxing was not possible for me right then. Old Kit loved to take nips of anything that grew beside the road, and she was very likely to get herself a bad case of colic by doing that. She needed to feel a firm hand on the reins, and to hear a firm voice whenever her head dipped to one side or the other to take a bite. Corn leaves were her favorite, and they also caused the worst colic. I was not sure what we would find at the little cottage in Lee, and so I did not want to be nursing Kit with colic all night.

As we rattled along with Sim sleeping peacefully, I thought about life as it was for us at that time. Pa's tailoring business should be as active as ever, with the fighting now in Boston and to the south, if what I heard was true. I wondered if the fighting moved further south than it was then, would the call for uniforms also go away? Pa had often said that uniform making would not last forever, and we should be thinking about what to make to replace the uniforms. I would enjoy making pretty gowns for women, but there was not much call for those in our small town and frontier lives. The linsey-woolsey that I wove for the uniform shirts would make good blankets, and two lengths of thirty six inch wide cloth would make a double bed width blanket. Sewing the lengths of cloth together was not hard, and such blankets would be easy to produce.

My thoughts turned to my Henry. "Henry is Henry," brother Thomas had said, and it was a good way to describe my husband. I loved him, missed him, but I accepted his restlessness. Something I had heard came to mind:

"If you love someone,
Let him go.
If he loves you,
He'll come back to you."

If Henry were meant for me, he would return. Meanwhile, all the skills that my Bickford relatives and Pa Tufts had taught me would help me to support Sim and myself. The fact that I could not own anything, or have a voice in how things in the world went, really did make me cross. However, I remembered my father's favorite advice to ". . . stand up straight and tall, look the world in the eye, and BE somebody".

Suddenly, I was not worrying about Baby Thomas, but I was looking ahead! I relaxed a bit, but not enough to doze, because Kit needed my firm hold on the reins, I knew.

As for Sim's future, I was so pleased that his Uncle Thomas liked him, and he liked his Uncle Tom and Aunt Liz. I hoped they would always get along as well, and that Sim would, in fact, play with Baby Thomas some day. As I considered it all, I knew that little Thomas would never really be part of my life, but I knew he would have a good life with Thomas and Elizabeth. I thought that Pa would agree with that idea, and I looked forward to telling him all about it.

While Thomas had a future, I thought, I must think about Sim's. He needed to begin learning and doing jobs around the farm. Pa had sheep, two cows, some goats, pigs, and a henhouse full of hens and roosters. Sim now needed to begin with chores like gathering eggs and tending to pigs and sheep to get him familiar with all of those farming chores. When I thought about my years learning about growing crops and animals, I remembered Buster. I decided that Sim needed a dog to care for, too. I would talk to Pa about all of these things, because this was the time for Sim to learn to be a responsible adult. I knew Pa would agree with that idea, too.

Sim awoke as if by magic as the little cottage in Lee on the Exeter Road came into sight. He stretched, yawned, and looked around to immediately recognize where we were.

"There's Pa's house, Mama! We're nearly there! Oh boy, Oh boy!"

"Yes, Sim, we're nearly there. Be sure to remember to be very quiet and to stay near me or near Pa until we see how things are in the house."

As we pulled up to the hitching post, I noticed that an addition was being made onto the back of the little cottage. I was anxious to know what that was all about. However, Kit needed our care, so we drove past the hitching bar to the barn and stopped in front of the big barn door. It had to be opened wider for us to drive in, so Sim and I jumped down and opened it together. Then I led Kit, still hitched to the wagon, into the big barn floor.

"Prince," Pa's other horse, nickered his greeting to Kit. They were an interesting mis-matched pair. Kit was a big horse, a deep roan colored mare, with a white strip down her forehead to her nose. Prince was a smaller, dappled gray gelding with very gentle ways. When Sim was just a toddler, Prince would allow him to run under his belly to cinch the harness, and he never swelled out his belly to keep the cinch loose when Sim fastened it. He and Sim were special friends, so I told Sim to measure out Prince's oat treat to have ready when we gave Kit hers.

When her harness was off, Kit shook with the pleasure. She was hot, even in the cool weather, and so we put on her blanket right away. I did not give her water before she had her oats treat. As soon as she was cooled off a bit, we gave her some water in a pail in her manger and plenty of hay from the mow. We did the same for Prince, and left them contentedly munching in their adjoining stalls.

At last, we took what remained of the lunch Elizabeth had packed for us, the pillow, the small packet of Sim's clothes, and headed for Pa's house. As we passed in back of the house, we got a better look at the ell. It was to be a good-sized room, I thought. We knocked on the door of the family living quarters, and heard Pa's welcome,

"Come on in!"

Sim ran to Pa and gave him a big hug at about the height of his knees. Then Pa knelt down for a hug and a kiss on the cheek. Then Pa stood up, gave me a brief hug, and took a long look at me. All he said was, "Tell me."

As I related everything that had happened in the past months, Pa listened with all of his attention. He nodded his head now and then, smiled now and then, and kept his eyes on my face the whole time. When I had finished, he said,

"Tell me truly, Lydia, is this the right decision? Did you have regrets all the way home? Do you feel that this was really the best thing for Baby Thomas?"

"I truly do, Pa. It was not easy to leave my babe in Northwood and to know that he will not be a part of my life, but I could not, in all truth, think of what might happen to him if I brought him back to Lee, and you know as well as I do that I have no other place to go and no one else who would be as kind to me as you are."

"Thank you for saying that, Lydia, and let me tell you how we will manage here with Mary in her condition."

Pa then told me about the ell being added to the house. He had found two girls just over from Ireland, and they would tend to Mary night and day. They would live with Mary in the ell and one of them would be with her at all times. There would be no more incidents like the one with Baby Thomas. For the time being, Hannah, Nancy, and Mary were to stay on the second floor of the cottage. Sim and I would sleep in the family room, and Pa would sleep in the tailor shop. I would cook for the three upstairs ladies for a few weeks, but as soon as the ell was done, complete with fireplace, the cooking for the three of them would be in the ell. I then would need to cook only for Sim, Pa, and myself.

Before our talk was over, Pa and I had touched on many things, including the future of the tailor shop. Pa's thinking on that had been similar to mine, but he suggested that we keep on thinking and talking about that for awhile, get caught up with present orders, and then maybe try new things to sell.

"You must be tired, Lydia, so I'll fry some bacon and eggs for our supper, and give you a taste of bread that I made myself! I've already taken some supper to the three ladies upstairs, so you won't have to do that. You may sleep on the settle, here, and Sim can have his pillow on the floor near you. We have plenty of blankets in the Shop. It won't be long until the room is ready for Mary and the girls, and then we can all stretch out a bit."

After we ate the good tasting supper Pa had cooked, we settled down for the night, and I could think again about my life. I gave a small prayer of thanks for my good luck in our lives with Pa. He was a good teacher, farmer, tailor, and human being. We would be all right, Sim and I.

That night I learned how to sleep on a settle. The seat is narrow, and so I would sit at about the middle of the settle, swing my legs up and to one side and then put my head down on the other side. I could sleep well by lying on my side, but the seat was too narrow to allow sleeping on my back. If I wanted to turn over, I sat up, reversed the position of my legs and head, and lay down on the other side. In spite of the activity involved in turning over, I slept well.

The next day Sim and I met Hannah and Nancy and said our greetings to Mary. Hannah was a large, red headed, green eyed Irish girl of about twenty, who loved to talk, and did that a lot. Nancy was smaller, about 25, with dark hair and hazel eyes. She was quieter, but smiled with her eyes as well as with her mouth. Both of the girls were kind to Mary, each in her own way. They called her "Dear," and tried to include her in their lively talk. Mary forgot to call me "Liedja," and to tell the story of how she gave me that name. With time and kind care, those unpleasant ways might leave her, I thought.

Since Hannah was on duty and Nancy was not, Nancy stayed below stairs with us and helped me to get the dinner we would have at noon. She was good help, and knew how to cook on a fireplace. We also made biscuits for baking in the brick oven to eat with the meat stew we set to cook over the fire.

Pa asked Sim to go with him to the barn to begin his lessons in farming. Sim skipped along at Pa's side as they went. I smiled, hoping this was a good beginning for Sim to learn skills he would use all of his adult life.

When they returned with a pail full of milk, we strained the milk through cheese cloth spread in a sieve, put some of the milk into smaller pails in the "cold" pantry, and put the rest of the milk into pans to let the cream rise. We would skim off the cream later and churn it into butter and use the skim milk to make cottage cheese by putting the milk into covered pans near the coals of the fire to curdle.

Sim followed me closely during the milk storage process, and Pa was smiling at the thought of again having cottage cheese and butter in the house. He went into the tailor shop as soon as he had washed his hands; Sim imitated Pa's every move and went into the tailor shop, too. Nancy and I sat a few moments and chatted by the fire.

"Where is your family now, Nancy?"

"They live in a small town called Ballinasloe, north and east of Limerick. I miss them, of course, but my life here is much better than it would be there. I hope they will someday come over, too, but they are very set in their ways, and they may not ever come to join me."

"Pa is a very wise and kind man. He has been very good to me and Sim, and he says we can stay with him as long as we want. I am most grateful. My husband, Henry, comes and goes. I never know when he might walk in the door. Has Pa told you about him?"

"Yes, he has, and he has told us not to pay any attention to him. You will tend to him. Does he often come home to you wounded?"

"He loves to wrestle, box, play knife games, and those things that young men do. I often have to try to bind up his wounds, but he usually doesn't stay until he's healed. He's very restless."

One day when Sim was helping Pa with the sheep, Sim came crying to me with a snake bite on his bare heel. He had not been watching where he stepped in the sheep fold, and he had stepped right onto the coiled snake. When he described the snake, I realized that it was a Garter snake, not poisonous, but it hurt, all the same, and it scared Sim. I cleaned up the wounded heel, put some vinegar-water into it, and bound it with a clean rag. Sim limped off, and I decided it was time to talk with Pa about a dog that would guard Sim from such accidents.

Soon Pa and I talked about a dog for Sim. I described my childhood Buster, and Pa knew right where he might get a similar Collie for Sim. In a few days, "Laddie" joined our family. He was a handsome blond Collie, with a pointed nose that he was good at sticking into anything that might be a danger to Sim. It was plain from the very first, Pa was Laddie's Master, and Sim was Laddie's Charge. The rest of the family were nice enough, especially when we fed him. but Laddie preferred to be with either his Master or his Charge.

Laddie was good at herding sheep, if either his Master or his Charge asked him to "Herd." No one else seemed to be able to find the right tone of voice with which to say, "Herd," and so he would sit down and look expectantly for either his Master or his Charge to tell him what to do!

Our lives settled into a regular routine and before we really thought much about time, it was 1779, soon to be 1780, and son Simeon Tufts was soon to be ten years old. He was becoming more blond, and his eyes were a deep shade of blue sometimes, but in the bright sunlight they became light blue "farmer's eyes," I called them.

My Henry was seldom at the little cottage in Lee, and that didn't seem to be a matter anyone found strange. One time he came to ask me for two linsey-woolsey shirts that he could take to his brother Eliphalet in West Point, New York, when he went there to visit him. Pa allowed that he approved, so I gave Henry the two shirts. I never knew whether his brother got them until I read Henry's book in 1808. In that book Henry described giving his brother the shirts—without saying where he got them.

Chapter 10

1780

Soon life at the tailor's cottage developed into a regular pattern. Pa was teaching Simeon the barn chores such as feeding the animals and cleaning out the stalls and pens. I taught him how to take care of the hen house and how to deal with the broody old hens. It was plain to see that Sim liked animals and liked caring for them. We marked the seasons by planting and harvesting cycles, as well as sheep shearing, butchering, and the rest of the annual chores of running a small farm. Simeon usually spent a few weeks each year during the early spring, when the tasks on our farm were at a low level, with his Uncle Tom, Aunt Liz, and Thomas. He came home after each visit more and more determined to be like his Uncle Thomas when he grew up. He loved to tell us about the things Uncle Tom had shown him that he needed to know when he settled new land into a farm. He really wanted to settle on some new land when he was old enough, he said.

Caring for Mary was done by the Irish girls, who soon proved their worth in other ways, too. As Pa and I explored ways to keep the tailoring business going in spite of fewer calls for uniforms, we talked with Nancy and Hannah about the fabric business in Ireland. Nancy was from the southern part of Ireland, and while weaving there was done in most homes, the fiber was usually flax to make beautiful Irish linen fabric.

Hannah was from the north, where Donegal tweed weaving of wool was done in most homes. The father of the family was often the weaver, and the mother and children prepared and spun the fleece for the weaving. It all sounded so easy when she described it, and yet the fabric was very new and different to us.

First of all, fleeces were dyed before spinning. Pa and I had, for the most part, dyed the yarn and thread after it was spun and was ready to weave, but for tweeds we would need many colors of washed and combed fleece to spin into the main color before it was woven. The rather lumpy and multicolored yarn then could be used as weft (the long way) or warp (the yarn in the shuttle that crossed the weft).

After trying many different ways of dressing the loom and winding the bobbins, I found my favorite way to weave tweed was to use the plain spun yarn for the long weft. After the weft was wound onto the loom and threaded through the heddles, then the specially spun tweed was wound onto the bobbins for the shuttle and worked back and forth over-and-under the weft.

I used a plain over-and-under weave, and so it was fast to make fabric.

For the first time, I tried dyeing the washed fleece before it was spun. By trying many different herbs, weeds, nuts, and even copper coins, I produced many different colors of fleece to make the small splashs of color in the tweed fabric. One of my favorites was the blue-green shades that were made from beechnut shells. At first, I did most of the spinning with a drop spindle, because I could control the tightness of the spin more easily, and incorporate the small bits of colored fleece into the spinning process more slowly. Finally, I was able to use the walking wheel and to spin the tweed yarn as fast as I could spin the plain yarn.

Hannah taught me about the use of the beater on the loom. She had learned much about weaving from her father, whom she called "My Da." By thoroughly crowding the warp threads tightly together, and then fulling the woven fabric by submerging it in very hot water, I could get a thick blanket fabric, almost like felt, that kept out winter's chilly winds well. Hannah told me that the "old" Irish way of fulling wool after it was woven included dumping the chamber pots into the boiling water, but I preferred the plain boiling water, with a little vinegar added if needed. I also made light-weight wool blankets and linsey woolsey very light-weight blankets for summer use. The weight of the finished fabric depended upon how many times I banged the beater against the warp, and how hard I banged it at each pull. I loved the learning, and the experimenting, too.

I also used the wool yarns I spun to knit socks, mittens, and warm sweaters for Pa, Mary, and Simeon. Both Nancy and Hannah were expert knitters. They made Irish Aran patterns that involved cables, crosses, ribs, bobbles, and many kinds of figures in their knitting. They preferred undyed yarn, so their sweaters were usually off-white in color, and they wanted most of the natural lanolin to remain in the yarn, so the fleece was washed clean, but not too much, and the sweaters were waterproof and very warm.

Local fishermen and lobstermen learned how useful Nancy and Hannah's Irish sweaters and mittens were to them, especially in the winter. They told us that when they got new mittens in the winter, they would dip them into the salt water and then let them freeze. The frozen mittens were very, very warm and they were waterproof, too. Soon, we devised a way to knit in small pieces of fleece, so the mittens were lined on the inside with the ends of fleece—another layer added to protect the men's hands from the cold icy water as they worked.

As the years slipped by, Simeon grew in size and knowledge, and I learned many things, too. In 1780, Sim became nine and a half years old. He was as tall as I was. The Revolutionary War had moved far to our south, and the orders for uniforms had decreased to nearly none. My blankets and the Irish girls' knits were becoming well known so we filled our stock shelves with those things. The sales of our goods combined with bartering for my services as mid-wife and nurse kept us in staples and Simeon's farming kept us in food.

Mary was becoming more and more feeble in mind as well as body. She seldom came into the little cottage from her room in the ell, and when she did, one of the Irish girls was always with her. They continued to be gentle and kind to her, and she did not become hysterical very often. Henry could upset her when he came, but his stays were brief, and she would soon settle down to being placid again after he left. Pa and the Irish girls could seem to understand her gibberish, but Sim and I could not. When Mary became bed-ridden, Nancy and Hannah were very busy with her care, and I began again to cook for them in the kitchen of the cottage. They seemed grateful, and praised the dishes that I sometimes concocted, especially Indian Puddings made with raisins, currents, dates, or nuts.

Mary died in her sleep in March, 1780. She was 58 years of age, and had been deranged for nearly forty of those years, since the still-birth of the only girl child born to her and Pa Tufts. Hannah and Nancy had come to love Mary, and they wept for her. I wept for Pa. He was lost without his Mary, even though it had been years since she had descended into herself. He was so lonely. He was six years older than Mary, and his health began to decline markedly. However, he remained kind to me and to Simeon.

Pa continued to help Sim with the farm work, and I became more and more in charge of the tailor shop. As his eyesight began to fail, Pa could do less and less in the shop, but he was still interested in it. He had very stiff joints, used a cane, and had difficulty walking, so he did less and less work outside. He still enjoyed planting a garden, so each spring he would sit on a box to plant the seeds. He was always supportive, and always had helpful suggestions about a weaving, spinning, or knitting idea, and seemed to enjoy talking about them.

One day, he said to me, "Lydia, you need, I think, to become more of a salesman for your work. Why not take some samples of your weaving and knitting to Portsmouth to show to some merchants? I know some shopkeepers there who might either buy some to re-sell, or rent you some shelf space to show your work. You could work out something, I think, even without my being there. I'll mind the shop. You could see if Hannah and Nancy would like you to find a way for them to sell their knitting, too."

"Oh, Pa, I don't think I could do that! I've never had to do much selling. I'd be so afraid of traveling to Portsmouth. That's how my father was killed, trying to protect farmers from Privateers. I don't know about going there!"

"I know about your father, Lydia. I heard about it at the time he was killed. But it is not so dangerous these days, and I know a boatman who would look out for you and Simeon. Sim is old enough and big enough to protect you now, and seeing Portsmouth city would be good for him as well as you."

Hannah had gone to work for a neighbor, but she still left sweaters in our shop to be sold.

Nancy was still with us. At the time of Mary's death, she told me she would stay with me until Pa did not need care any more. I was grateful for that, because the tailor shop, the cooking, and helping Pa amounted to a two-person set of jobs. Simeon was doing nearly all of the farm work, and he was busy with that.

During several more talks about it, Pa gave me some names of merchants in Portsmouth who might be interested in our products. He advised me about prices to ask, and different kinds of agreements I could make with the merchants. I felt I would be more comfortable if I bought the knitted items from the Irish girls, paying them a fair price, and then re-sold them to the Portsmouth merchants. Then, if anything happened to the knit goods, the Irish girls would have their money.

The boatman was Captain John Follett, a neighbor I knew well. The Captain told me all about how we would make the trip, and so as time went by, I became easier in my mind about it all. We would sort our goods into bundles that we could load onto a four wheeled wagon that Sim would push when we got to Portsmouth. We wrapped each type of item separately in bundles covered in oiled cloth to protect the fabrics from rain or splashing water during the boat trip.

One bright sunny morning in October, 1780, when the tide was high in Great Bay, Sim and I set off with Capt. Follett in his big double-ended dory. In addition to the Captain, there were four oarsmen, Simeon, and me. We had 20 blankets of different weights, 20 Irish Aran sweaters, and 25 pairs of mittens, some with fleece lining, in addition to a bundle of socks and scarves. On top of it all was the four-wheeled wagon, upside down. I had made new outfits for both Sim and me. He had a new shirt and pants, and I had a new linsey-woolsey dress. Sim's shirt was dyed from beechwood shells and was light blue linsey-woolsey. It was as blue as his eyes and set off his blond hair well. His pants were off the rack of uniforms—it gave me a start when I saw that a men's size small fitted him well. They were tan knee-length, and his stockings were knitted off-white in an Irish pattern. He had new black shoes from the cobbler, too. My dress was blue, to match my eyes, Nancy said. I made a white collar and cuffs and hair cover of linen trimmed with some hand crocheted lace that Nancy made for me. Both of us had long hooded capes of dark wool in case of bad weather. We both felt very special in our new clothes. Pa gave us both hugs and wished us well.

"You can do it, Lydia, I know you can," Pa said, when we went to him to say goodbye.

I wasn't so sure, but I lifted up my head and once more thought of my father's advice. As we left Pa standing by the hitching bar in front of the little cottage, I told myself to "Sit up tall and BE somebody" once more.

Old Kit pulled Sim and me in our loaded wagon to the wharf in Newmarket on Great Bay. She would be boarded in Mr. Frost's stable while we were gone. After we had crossed Great Bay, we entered the Piscataqua River. The rowers could "lock" their oars when we were on the River, because the tide was going out, and we could feel it pulling us fast down-River along with it. Other than steering to avoid other boats, sand bars, or going too fast, the oarsmen could rest while we were headed down the River. After a while, we saw many buildings appearing on our right as we sped along. We were approaching Portsmouth! Capt. Follett showed me Badger's Island, which was part of the unsettled Northern Province of Massachusetts, called Kittery, on our left. Straight ahead, I saw many tall masts. Those, he told me, were anchored at the ship-building yard just off Badger's Island.

In Portsmouth, we would stay in a rooming house for a few nights until we had finished visiting the list of merchants Pa had given me, shown samples of our wares, and made business deals, we hoped, with one or two of them. After the Captain had docked our boat, his men helped Sim unload our goods onto the four-wheeled wagon that was now on the wharf. I watched the work as I prepared myself for the big city and fast-paced life there. When the wagon was loaded, the Captain helped me climb up the narrow gangplank onto the wharf. He gave us directions to the rooming house Pa had specified, which was in "Strawberry Banke", an old section of the city very close to the wharf and to the merchants we needed to visit.

"Just go down along the River bank for about a quarter mile, and you will see a sign with a big strawberry on it. It will say 'Strawberry Stay.' Tell them that your Pa Tufts and I sent you. The owner is Mr. Oscar Leighton. He will treat you well."

Mr. Leighton greeted us kindly with a smile. After stowing the loaded wagon in Mr. Leighton's office, Sim and I were shown to a room with a trundle bed on the second floor and told that tea would be served in about an hour—it was then 3:30 in the afternoon. I was glad to lie on the soft featherbed, covered with my cape for a few minutes, as Sim pulled the trundle bed out from under my bed and fell asleep on it right away. It had been an exciting day for us both.

Chapter 11

1780 – Portsmouth

At 4:30 in the afternoon on our first day in the New Hampshire capitol city of Portsmouth, Sim and I were roused from our short naps by the tinkle of a bell, and our host's voice below stairs saying, "Tea is served, tea is served."

We went down toward the sound, were greeted by Mr. Leighton and directed to our left at the foot of the stairs. There we found a large dining room with a long table in the middle and smaller tables around the sides of the room. The big table in the middle was set up with place settings all around and platters of food.

"Welcome to High Tea at the 'Strawberry Stay'," said our host. "We serve a High Tea each afternoon at 4:30, and we hope you will join us whenever your schedule allows."

As Sim and I found places and sat at the table, we had to admire the feast that had been set out for us. There were cranberry scones hot from the oven, cold meat sandwiches, dainty cucumber sandwiches, cakes and cookies and many other good looking things to eat. We found that we were both hungry from our trip, and so we did justice to the bountiful table. As we ate, Mr. Leighton, who sat with us, poured our tea with great ceremony, but ate little, told us about his life and family. He started out by telling us where the name "Strawberry Banke" came from. When English explorers first saw this area, long before the Pilgrims came to settle in Plymouth Massachusetts, they were struck by the rich beds of strawberries that grew all around the natural harbor, and thus named it "Strawberry Banke."

He himself was from a family of "hoteliers," he said, and he and his brothers and sisters all enjoyed the business of providing shelter and food for travelers. One of his relatives even ran a small inn during the summer months on "Old Smutty Nose," one of the Isles of Shoals that lie about 10 miles off the coast of New Hampshire and Maine. Another relative was the lighthouse keeper on the same island, and his wife and children helped to run the small inn there.

Mr. Leighton told us he was interested in our purpose in coming to Portsmouth, I hoped that my discomfort in the City was not obvious, but if it was, it was, I thought. When we told Mr. Leighton why we were there, he asked to see some of our wares. As soon as he looked at and touched the Irish knits, especially the mittens, he asked for prices of the items. The sweaters were to be fifteen pounds each for all sizes except very large, which would be eighteen pounds. He said that he would like to tell his relatives on Old Smutty Nose about them. There were many fishermen and lobstermen based out there who could use such items, he thought.

Mr. Leighton also asked whom we intended to see in Portsmouth. I mentioned some of the names Pa Tufts had given me, including a Mr. Remick on the corner of Congress and Market Streets. Mr. Leighton wanted to see the blankets, and seemed as pleased with them as with the Irish knits. We were encouraged.

We began to feel sleepy with our full stomachs and exciting day behind us, and so we bade Mr. Leighton "Good Night."

He replied, "Tomorrow, breakfast will be served from 7:00 AM until 9:00. Most of the stores you named will open about 9:00, so you can be on the doorstep first thing. Will you have Tea with me tomorrow afternoon?"

We thanked him, and said we would be back by afternoon Teatime, we were sure.

Both Sim and I fell asleep soon after we settled into our room. Even the unfamiliar city noises of horses' hooves clopping on the cobblestones and the ringing of the bell buoys and boat bells did not disturb our sleep.

Refreshed, we ate well the substantial breakfast that awaited us at the dining room table. It was as bountiful as the Tea had been the day before, and we relished it all. Scones hot from the oven again, oatmeal, and bacon and eggs among other items.

We set off down Congress Street to Main Street to find Mr. Remick, who owned a dry goods store at the corner of Main and Market Streets. Mr. Remick was in his store, and receiving salesmen, he said. Simeon wheeled the barrow right into the store, and we began to show him our goods. He stopped my nervous fast talking with:

"Mrs. Tufts, please stop for a moment. I want to get my fellow merchants to come and hear you, and then you won't have to deliver your message too many times. How does that sound?"

That was a relief. Sim and I sat down for a few minutes, and then several gentlemen came in Mr. Remick's front door. He introduced each one, and mentioned where his store was located nearby.   There was Mr. Forbes, Mr. Boothby, Mr. Foss, and Mr. Rowland.

"Now we are all here, Mrs. Tufts, and you can tell us all at once your story. First, I would like to tell my fellow dry goods storekeepers a little about you both. This is the daughter-in-law and grandson of our old friend, Henry Tufts the Tailor, of Lee. Sadly, he has lost his wife Mary recently. Young Mrs. Tufts has lived with her father-in-law and helped him with his business for about ten years. During the last several years, Mary was quite ill. Mrs. Lydia and Simeon have learned much from Henry, who is now feeble with old age. She will tell you about her handwoven blankets and about her Irish knits."

First, I showed them all the heavy Donegal tweed blankets, then the light-weight blankets, some of them tweed, and then the linsey-woolsey blankets, which were dyed different colors, but none were tweed. I gave the price of each blanket as I showed it to them and let them feel it. I had decided to ask eighteen pounds for the heavy double-bed sized blankets, The medium weight blankets were to cost twelve pounds for a double size. The Linsey-woolsey blankets were eight pounds each. Single bed sizes were less, of course. Each store owner felt each blanket, and hefted it to test its weight. I answered their questions about how many blankets we had with us, what sizes they were, how fast they were to make, how I took orders, and so forth.

Then, Sim unwrapped the bundle of Irish knits made by the girls. The men felt them, and felt the slightly slippery feel of the lanolin in the sweaters. They sniffed them for the distinctive smell of the lanolin, and nodded their heads when I said that fishermen and lobstermen liked those items for their work, especially during the winter months. Each man examined each sweater as thoroughly as he had the blankets. Then we went to the mittens; they interested the dry goodsmen, too. I answered further questions about how we made the "stuffed fleece" mittens with the extra layer of fleece on the inside, gave them the price for each item, and finally I showed them the hats, stockings, and scarves some with Aran patterns, too. Sim was glad to show them his stockings, and did such good modeling that the men clapped their hands. They had many questions about how fast I could fill orders and how many items I would leave there with them. They asked if I wanted cash. And of course I said "Yes." They smiled at that, and said they would talk together about it all and get in touch with me at the "Strawberry Stay" later that day.

Sim and I left, very tired and tense and a little encouraged. As we headed for the "Strawberry

Stay," we decided that we should see some more of the city while we were there. Sim wheeled the barrow into Mr. Leighton's office, and we set out to see Portsmouth.

We walked back to Congress Street, and this time looked around us. One of the first things we noticed as we walked slowly along was that in the Strawberry Banke section of the city, many of the lawns around the houses and other buildings had wild strawberry plants growing behind the white picket fences that surrounded most of the buildings. As we looked straight down Congress Street, we saw a mansion at the other end that looked very elegant. It was 2 stories high, made of red brick with white painted wood trim. On top of the second story, a white rail went all around the eaves, and each window and door had a curved archway of white wood above it.

"Let's go nearer and see that nice mansion," I said to Sim, who nodded his agreement. The fence around this mansion was at least six feet high, with an archway above double gates. A plate on the fence said it was the Governor's Mansion. At that time, the second Governor appointed by the King of England was living there. His name was John Wentworth, nephew of the very unpopular Benning Wentworth. As we got nearer to the building, the white gates opened, and six or eight men, elegantly dressed in shiny satin clothes with white wigs under their tri-con hats, and mounted on prancing horses, came out of the gate. One of the men had a white cockade in his tri-con, and I realized that he was John Wentworth himself. Ahead of the men a black man in a dark blue uniform riding a donkey shouted as he rode,

"Hear, ye, Hear ye, Governor John Wentworth is out for his daily ride. Hail and step aside! Hail and step aside!"

Sim and I stepped as far out from the Street as we could get to let them by. As they drew nearer, I caught my breath. The Governor was riding my dear "On'ry!" I knew it! I could not believe my eyes, but there he was, prancing as when he was a young colt carrying my father. His muzzle was white, but his neck was in a perfect "tuck" and his rear legs danced to the drum beat that only he heard. Before I thought about what I was doing, I shouted,

"On'ry, On'ry, my dear On'ry!"

His ears flicked down and to the sides, and he did his little sideways fast-step. The Governor's hat and wig were badly dislocated, but he kept his seat. He did not have time to look my way, for which I was grateful, and 'On'ry' soon went back to his usual rhythm. It all happened so fast that I didn't understand why the Governor whipped poor 'On'ry' so hard, right in his tender spots. 'On'ry' laid back his ears at the whipping but was on his way forward in no time. I felt badly that I had thoughtlessly caused him a whipping.

When it was all over, and the men had ridden down the Street, Sim asked me who 'On'ry' was.

"'On'ry' was my father's horse when I was a little girl; I loved that horse, and I learned to ride on him. He was always skittish, like you saw him then, and so my father, your Grandfather, Ben Bickford, was the only one in our family who was

111

allowed to ride him. After my father was killed, I never knew what happened to his horse. Just before he died, I begged and begged my father to let me ride 'On'ry', mostly because he was so frisky, and he was a challenge. My father taught me a good lesson along with how to ride. He taught me that when things seem too much, you ". . .just straighten up your back bone, lift up your head, and BE somebody."

Sim and I headed back down Congress Street and this time we turned onto Market Street. We turned to our left, which would take us down to the river front. We saw many pubs and drinking places along the Street. There were horses tied to hitching posts all along on both sides. Many people were walking on the sides of the Street, some milling aimlessly. We had planned to watch the busy River with boats going every which-way. Suddenly, there in front of me stood my husband, Henry, with a woman on each arm. They were going from one drinking place to another, I guessed, because Henry was very unsteady on his feet.

"Well, well, if it isn't my two Cerulean Beauties! Don't you look rich in your blue to match your eyes! You're growing big, Simeon, and you're looking well, Lydia. Tell me, why are you in our City?"

After I got back my breath and could speak, I replied, " We're here to sell some things from the Tailor shop, Henry, and we will be returning to Lee today."

"I don't see any goods from the Tailor Shop. Does that mean you have some money?'

"No money, Henry, and no goods, either. If you want to see your father again while he lives, you'd do well to come to Lee to see him soon. He's not well. For now, it's goodbye to you, Henry. We must be ready for our boat to sail." We headed for the waterfront.

"Mom, why did you tell Father that we're going home today? We can't go until we sell our things!"

"Sim, your father is always looking for money from me or from your Pa. He never has any to share with you or me, though. This time, I cannot give him money. We need our money to pay for our room and meals, even if we don't sell any of our goods."

We wound our way back to the 'Strawberry Stay'. By the time we reached our lodging, I had recovered from my glimpse of Henry and his way of life, and my heart had slowed down to a regular beat. In spite of his ways I still loved him, and I wished so very much that he could live in a different way. As I calmed down, I talked with Sim about his father's way of living, and I stressed that it was not my way, and I hoped it never would be Sim's way. He promised me he would never live like his father did. He promised me to be more like his Uncle Thomas when he grew up.

He asked me, "Why did you marry a man like my father and not a man like Uncle Thomas?"

I could not answer him in a way that would satisfy him at age nine and a half or ten, but I promised to talk later with him about the matter, and he seemed satisfied with that. We had arrived at the "Strawberry Stay," and another High Tea, we knew, was waiting for us.

Mr. Leighton told us that he had heard from his relatives on Smutty Nose, and they would be interested in displaying some of our goods. They would like to sell them for the prices that I had quoted to Mr. Leighton, and they would charge me 10% of the price we got per item for the display space. I thanked him, and told him that I would have to wait until Mr. Remick from Market Street contacted me with the results of this morning's meeting.

Before I could ask him how he had heard so quickly from Old Smutty Nose, he explained that fishermen came into Portsmouth daily from the Isles, and so communication was very steady and very fast.

In fact, he said, our Tea today would have some of the "catch" the fisherman had brought to sell to Mr. Leighton. In addition to the hot scones, we had delicious lobster salad sandwiches and clam chowder. Tomorrow, Mr. Leighton promised, there would be some oyster fritters for our Tea.

As we were finishing our tea, there was a knock on the door of the house, and an envelope was delivered to me. In the envelope was a letter that I excused myself from the table to read in our upstairs room.

Sim followed me to our room in a few minutes, and he saw the tears in my eyes and said, "Is it bad news, Mom?"

"No, Sim it is the most wonderful news it could be. Mr. Remick and the other dry goods men we met want to buy all we have brought with us, and they also want to place orders for more of our goods. The news couldn't be better!"

I was glad that Pa Tufts had made sure I had a complete list of all the goods we had brought, and had added the prices up so I knew ahead of time how much money I should be paid for all of it, or for part of it, or however it turned out. I sorted through the papers in the leather pouch that was always on my arm to find the list. It totaled 850 Pounds, more money than I ever thought could possibly be in one place! My next problem was how to ask for the pay: Should I carry that much money with me?

Not very safe.

Should I ask for a bank draft?

Safer, not surer, in these crazy money times.

I needed some advice, and quickly. Sim and I talked about it, and he agreed with me that Mr. Leighton seemed to be honest and wise. We would ask him, but in the morning.

Chapter 12

1780

After the night's good rest, things didn't look as complicated to me. I realized that I still had not answered Mr. Leighton about sending some of our goods to his relatives on Old Smutty Nose, but I really wanted to sell our things outright and not put them on display. I decided that, for the time being, I would not speak to him about financial things, but go to Mr. Remick to hear about his offer. He had told us in the letter that he would be in his store at 9:00 AM, and would look forward to talking business with us then.

After another good, hearty breakfast, Simeon and I walked to Mr. Remick's store. Sim was pushing the barrow loaded with our goods, and I was thinking about how to talk with Mr. Remick and the other businessmen.

Mr. Remick greeted us pleasantly, and we sat down with him around a big table to make final agreements. He told us his merchant friends had asked him to settle with me, and then they would work things out with him and the goods we had in the barrow would be divided among them. He began: "Mrs. Tufts, you said yesterday that you wanted cash for your goods, and I can understand that. However, my figures, which are not final of course, come to nearly 1,000 pounds, and all of us together do not have that much cash. Are you willing to barter for some of your goods?"

I smiled. Familiar as I was with bartering, I could handle that method of payment in a comfortable way. I relaxed a bit, looking forward to the familiar process.

"I would be glad to barter for some of the goods, Mr. Remick. What do you have in mind?"

"What my fellow dry goods salesmen and I would like to do is pay you cash for the blankets. That would come to about 250 pounds. Then, for the knitted goods, we have access to very fine fleeces. We could offer you clean fleeces in payment for all of the knits. My figures show that you would have around 600 pounds' worth of fleeces, and that is a lot of fleece, but we could ship those you cannot take with you. How does that sound?"

I liked the sound of that offer. The Irish girls liked to spin the yarn for their knitting work, and as long as the fleeces were clean but still had some lanolin left in them, the girls would take the fleeces in partial payment for their work, I knew. I listed my conditions: "That sounds workable to me, Mr. Remick. I must insist that the fleeces be washed clean and be free of twigs and such. However, they must have lanolin remaining in them—that is what makes the sweaters waterproof. I think the fairest way to decide how much fleece an item is worth is to weigh the item, and then we can know how much fleece was used to make it."

Mr. Remick agreed to those terms. After weighing and discussions, we came to agreement on the following: one sweater equaled five pounds of fleece. One pair of stuffed mittens equaled one and one-half pounds of fleece. One pair of unstuffed mittens equaled one pound of fleece. One pair of long stockings equaled one pound of fleece. One scarf equaled one pound of fleece. By multiplying over and over, we came to the weight of fleece that would be owed to us. It was a lot! The twenty sweaters would require one hundred pounds of fleece alone!

Mr. Remick could get a hundred pounds of fleece to us at the waterfront by the next day, and the remaining sixty pounds would be shipped to us in Lee within the week . The cash for the blankets I would carry in a purse hidden under my clothing. The merchants placed orders for more blankets, some of which we had in the Tailor Shop, and for more sweaters as well. Mr. Remick would use Captain Follett to get future messages to me about goods he and his friends might want to buy.

As Sim and I returned to "Strawberry Stay" much later when all our business was over, I began to think about what Pa would say when he heard what I had agreed to. As we entered the "Stay," I asked Mr. Leighton to get word to Capt. Follett that we would be ready to go home to Lee the next day and that one hundred pounds of wool fleece would be at the wharf waiting for him to pick up to take with us. I also asked Mr. Leighton to have the bill for our lodging ready, and I would pay him either later today or tomorrow morning when we said our goodbyes.

"The tide will be running high at about 11:00 AM tomorrow. Capt. Follett will want to take it as it is on the rise to get up the River, so you'll need to be at the wharf by 9:00," Mr. Leighton advised us. "Maybe you would like to get your bill paid this afternoon. I'll see to it."

It was time to talk with Mr. Leighton about the knitted goods, and so I told him that Mr. Remick had bought all of them outright. I suggested he talk with Mr. Remick to make arrangements with him for displaying some items at the Isles of Shoals. He seemed to agree with that.

Our "High Tea" later that afternoon was very special. Mr. Leighton had the promised oyster fritters prepared, the usual delicious hot scones, more lobster salad sandwiches, and the cakes and cookies as well. There were several other guests in attendance at that Tea, and so we passed a pleasant afternoon on our last day in the capitol city of Portsmouth. It hadn't been such a bad experience, after all. My father's advice had helped me to get through it all, as usual. I thought, "I REALLY WAS somebody!"

After Mr. Leighton was paid and we were getting ready for bed, Simeon asked me if I would be glad to see the little Tailor's cottage in Lee once again. He was ready, he said, to go home.

"It's nice to see different sights and hear different sounds, but Home is best," he said as he drifted off to sleep. I certainly agreed with him, and I said a little "Thank you" prayer for our three days of a safe adventure.

We were ready for breakfast at 7:00 o'clock the next day, and we arrived at the water front well before 9:00 AM. Capt. Follett greeted us, and showed us the loaded fleeces in the stern of his big dory.

As the boatmen cast off and began to row up River, Simeon said, "Goodbye, Portsmouth, we'll come back again some day, I hope."

The trip up the River took longer than the trip down had, so it was afternoon before we entered Great Bay and headed for Newmarket. We shared the lunch Mr. Leighton had thoughtfully prepared for Sim and me with the oarsmen and Capt. Follett. The Capt. invited Sim to take a turn at the oars, and Sim decided he would enjoy settling a new farm more than he would like being a boatman when he grew up.

The fleeces were unloaded on the dock at Newmarket, and Kit and the wagon were soon retrieved from the boarding stable. As I paid our bill at the stable, Simeon loaded the wagon, and then picked me up for the ride to Lee. Kit knew we were heading home, and her head was high as she pulled the wagon along the road at a trot. She needed the firm hand on the reins, because she saw many delicious things to eat along the way. We all were in high spirits to be heading home.

Chapter 13

1780 – 1784

We soon came to the little house in Lee, and Simeon asked to take Kit to the barn after we had unloaded the fleece in the Tailor Shop.

"That would be a great help, Sim, as long as you put on your barn boots first. You don't want horse dung all over your good 'city shoes.'"

Sim replied, "Yes, Mom," in a way that didn't show much agreement with my concern for his shoes. However, he obeyed.

When we could settle down to speak with Pa, I told him all about the business plans I had made with Mr. Remick. Pa smiled and nodded his head. He said, "You've got a tall order to fill, Lydia, but I'm sure you can do it. I will help you in every way I can."

The fall of 1780 and the new year of 1781 would always be in my memory as a time of very long hours of work at the loom, at the spinning wheel, and with fleece and flax. I was able to produce the blankets Mr. Remick had ordered; the Irish girls knitted the sweaters, hats, mittens, and scarves that had been ordered, too.

Capt. Follett came to the tailor shop to get the items when they were ready, and returned in a few days with payment. Mr. Remick and I continued the practice of cash payment for the blankets and bartered payment in fleeces for the knitted items. Pa and I paid Hannah and Nancy partially in money and the rest in fleece. It seemed to be a satisfactory arrangement all around.

Sim took on more and more of the farm work, as Pa became more and more feeble. The spring of 1781 was the last year Pa was able to plant a garden. Sim shadowed him, and seemed to soak in everything Pa taught him. Sim had spent the usual time with his Uncle Tom and Aunt Liz, and reported to Pa, Nancy and me that Thomas was growing big and strong. Simeon was still learning land-settling skills from his Uncle, and his aim was still to settle some new land when he was old enough. He knew that at age ten he was still too young, but he was gaining on "old enough" every year, he said.

About a year after we had seen Henry in Portsmouth, he appeared at the little cottage in Lee. He professed to have had some very hard luck, no money of course, and he was without much clothing except the few thin summer clothes he wore. However, he carried with him some heavy velvet fabric. He asked if I would make him a warm under-suit, since winter was coming, of the velvet. Henry was gracious in all he did and said. He was kind and respectful to his father, supportive and helpful to Simeon and his farm work, and courtly toward me. At first, I gave Henry only short answers, as I remembered the scene on Market Street in Portsmouth just one year before. In time, I found his courtly manners very difficult to resist. After all, he was a human being, and I did love to see his eyes smile. He was sharing my bed before I gave the whole matter much thought.

One day during the three weeks or so that Henry was with us, Simeon asked me about his father.

"Is father here to stay with us? He is good help, and I like to talk to him as we work. He doesn't tell me much about his life, though. He does talk about some of the places he has been, and he's been everywhere!"

"I never know how long your father will be with us. I'm sure he will be here until I have his winter clothes done for him, but beyond that time, I can't be sure."

The pressure to weave, spin, card fleece, and prepare flax took so much thought and planning that I did not notice my November courses were long overdue. It was December, the weather was very cold; snow covered the ground when we discovered Henry was gone. He simply disappeared one day, along with a few pounds that I kept in the Shop to make change when a customer paid for a purchase. I wept a few tears, because it had been wonderful to have him with us. Pa didn't say much, but I knew he missed him, too.

We were less mindful of the Revolutionary War in those days, as the fighting had moved far to the south. There was even talk of peace being made with England, and freedom for us from English rule.

In February of 1782, Simeon made his yearly visit with his Uncle and Aunt. His little brother was six years old, and Sim returned full of stories of their playing and working for Uncle Tom together. Shortly after he returned to Lee, Sim gave me a squinty-eyed look and said,

"Mom, Aunt Liz says she's going to have a baby before long, and you are beginning to have a belly like hers. Are you going to have a baby?"

I knew that it was time for a talk with Sim, so we sat down together and I told him about how it is between a man and a woman when they love each other. I tried to answer the hard question he had asked me when we were in Portsmouth about why I married a man like Henry and not a man like Thomas.

"You see, Simeon, when love happens to a man or a woman, no thought is given about what kind of a person you are loving. It just happens, and you have to make the most of it and do what needs to be done. Your father is not a good provider, but I love him, and I can provide what is needed for you and me and Pa, so I do. My answer to you is, yes, I am going to have another baby. It will be in the summer, probably July, and so you will have a new brother or sister. Time will tell which it will be. Meanwhile, we need to keep working to make goods to sell and to help Pa in his old age."

Pa coached Sim well about what to plant where in the garden that spring, and Sim listened and followed his advice well. Pa understood about how to plant a different crop on a given piece of ground each year so as not to wear out the soil. Nancy continued to do most of the care for Pa, to help me with cooking now and then, and to knit sweaters, hats, scarves, and mittens. Hannah visited us often with her knitting, and the business was going well.

We began to hear more about peace with England, and Yorktown became a known place in Virginia to us. Spring became summer, and I became very heavy. I also began to feel the heat. Sweat ran down my back most of the time, and dripped from my forehead. I kept a "sweat rag" at the loom because weaving made the sweating worse. We heard word that Elizabeth and Thomas had a baby girl in Northwood. They named her "Lydia." We prepared for me to give birth, too. Remembering Baby Thomas's birth, I attempted to work up enough blankets to tide us over during my weeks of necessary bed rest. Nancy and Hannah would help me when I gave birth, and so I felt at ease as the early signs of delivery occurred on July 6, 1782.

By nightfall, a healthy baby girl, whom I named Deborah for my dear Aunt Deb, was with us. I slept soundly that night, waking only to feed little Deb when either Hannah or Nancy brought her to me.

The next morning, when Deborah had finished the first feeding of the day, I asked to keep her with me for a few minutes. When I helped with birthings, I always called this a mother's "taking stock" time. As I rubbed my hand over the baby's soft, soft skin on hands, feet, arms, and little legs, I said a thankful prayer. She was all there; her fingers were perfect, her tiny buds of toes were complete with nails that were thin as paper. I talked to her in my mind.

"Dear Baby Deborah, may you grow up to be like your Great Aunt, Deborah Reyes Bickford. She was strong, but sweet in nature, wise in thought, but her words were few. She meant that I should have a much easier life than I have chosen, but when I chose not to abide by her advice, she never said, "I told you so!" I loved her dearly, as I love you already. I promise to teach you all I know about the ways of this world; to believe in God; to walk with your back straight, your head up, and to BE somebody!"

As I day-dreamed away, I realized that I had not been able to "take stock" in this way with either Simeon or Baby Thomas. When Simeon was born, I was too worried about how both he and I could eat. With Baby Thomas, I needed to protect his very life, and had no time to think about his future. However, Simeon was my pride and joy, and I was able, with Pa's help and support, to provide for him and me and to help him, thus far, to know the ways of the world. Baby Thomas, thanks to Brother Thomas and Elizabeth, was having a good life, too. I felt blessed with all of that. I said a thanks to God. The Sunday Meeting house was quite a distance from the Tailor Shop, so I did not attend services regularly. However, I lived my faith as well as I could where I was.

Because I was able to rest without fears or worries, my strength came back after Deborah's birth in a very short time. I was soon seated at the loom, and as fall approached, I began to pick the herbs and flowers to make the winter's dyes. Simeon continued with harvest, Hannah went back to her employer's, and Nancy and I settled into a comfortable routine with the care of Pa and the Shop.

Simeon loved to rock the baby's cradle with his foot as he read to us in the evening. Pa enjoyed watching her little face for changes, and she seemed to respond to the adoring family around her.

One day, Pa said, "I sure would like to see that baby walk, but I don't expect to, Lydia. Are you ready, as I am, for me to go? I mean, is there any thing I can help you with?"

The tears welled up so fast that I could not reply for a few minutes. "Dear Pa, I don't know what we would do without your wisdom and kindness. You have been so good to Sim and me, ever since you and Mary took us in so long ago. I cannot think of life without you."

"Well, Lydia, you must think and make plans. As you know, according to the law, Thomas will inherit this house and everything in it. There is nothing I can do to change that. I know that you do now, but I encourage you to save, save, save, for the time when I am no longer here. I will speak to Thomas about letting you stay here, but I cannot promise that he will, or what he will do with the tailoring tools. I hope they will be yours, as they would be if I could give them to you."

"Thank you, Pa. You have always been generous to Sim and me. Is there anything that you would like Nancy to have when you no longer need it? Anything for Hannah?"

"I will think on that, Lydia, and let you know."

It was so typical of Pa that he would be concerned about Simeon and me and Nancy and Hannah as he faced his death. He was such a wise and honest man, that I began to grieve for him even before he died.

Pa went peacefully to his final sleep early in December, 1782. Simeon was eleven years old and Deborah was not yet six months old. One of the many things I grieved for Pa about was that my Deborah would never really remember him as she grew.

Shortly after Pa was laid to rest, Thomas made his visit to the little cottage in Lee. As usual, he was kind and spoke few words.

"Lydia, Elizabeth and I want you to know how much we appreciate all that you have done for both Mother Mary and for our Pa Tufts. Their final years in both cases were better because you were here with them. Liz and I are blessed with young Thomas as a member of our family, and we are grateful to you for allowing him to come to us seven years ago.

"Because of all that you have done for them, we want you, Sim, and Deborah to remain here, running the business as you have been doing for some years now. We hope that you will consider the animals, the tools, everything here to be yours, even though you cannot own it. We have our live stock and tools and all that we need in Northwood. Of course, I will be listed as "owner" here, but that is in name only. Please believe that."

There was the powerlessness of a woman again, I thought. However, I was blessed once more by Pa's thinking ahead and planning for me and my children. I thanked Thomas from the bottom of my heart. I offered to pay rent, but he declined that. I offered some blankets, and he accepted those for himself and his growing family in Northwood. I asked if Simeon could come and talk with us and hear the news himself. Thomas agreed, and together we told Sim that we would be staying in Lee and carrying on the business and the farm. He was joyful, and hugged his Uncle Thomas very hard.

After Thomas had left for Northwood, I called Nancy into the tailor shop for a talk. She had been nervous about Thomas's visit, as she knew well Pa's concern for all of us. Sim and I told her our good news. She clapped her hands with joy, and asked what we would like her to do. She had been with us for years, and we could not dismiss her, so we asked her to stay on with us and help with the cooking and housework, continue to knit up a storm, and maybe learn some other fiber skills. She agreed to stay for her room and board and a few pence a week to add to her pay for the knitting. She said she could manage on that, providing she might do a birthing now and then. All was agreed, and we settled down to a slightly different routine life.

1783 slipped into 1784. Simeon became twelve years old, nearer to his "Old Enough" years, he said. He was taller now than I, and

Deborah began to walk. Watching her, I missed our Pa. We did not see Henry until the fall of 1784. The usual rumors were delivered to us by the neighbors; that Henry was in this jail, had broken out of that jail, was in Vermont, in Virginia, in New York, had been arrested in Massachusetts, and so on. Now that the War was over, he was not being chased as a deserter, however.

Chapter 14

1784 ~ 1792

As our Deborah grew into a little girl, she became more a member of our family. She had serious, grave ways about her, but she was not grouchy, just serious about things. She loved to tag after Simeon as he did the farm chores, and as soon as she was big enough to do them, he gave her little jobs of her own. She did those in her usual grave way, and soon was coping with the broody hens very well indeed. Her first words were names of the animals, and she loved to say, "seep" for sheep, and so on. She was our joy. With blue eyes and brown hair, she was a pretty little girl.

Nancy, Hannah, and I continued to weave and knit. Orders for more goods came quite regularly from Mr. Remick, and after we had been to Portsmouth, I cleaned my linsey-woolsey blue dress to hang in the shop. We began to get orders for women's dresses similar to it. I kept a small amount of money in the shop till, but I also kept some in a "money belt" that I wore constantly. I remembered Pa's advice, and told no one where most of our savings were hidden.

I had pondered many hours about different places to hide it away from Henry's experienced and roving hands. Loose bricks in the fireplace were quick for him to spot, as were other places I thought about. However, I had worked long hours for that money, and I would not reveal to anyone where I hid it. I checked it only when I knew Henry was not around, and so our savings grew safely during the years we lived in the little cottage in Lee. Simeon had been a great help in earning the money, and I always remembered that fact. He ran errands, carried goods to Capt. Follett, and was always helpful in any way he could be.

Henry visited us now and then for short times, when he needed something—new clothes, money, courage, and so on. He seemed to have unlimited amounts of bad luck. It was always the same story. He had no money for us, was terribly sorry, and needed this or that or something else to ". . .tide him over," so that he could become a success and support us. I could remain cold to him for a few days, but then my defenses wore down and he shared my bed. The results were quite predictable: Our Hannah was born in April of 1785.

Named for my dear Irish friend, Hannah was a lovely blonde baby girl with azure blue eyes that glowed from the moment of her birth. She was also our joy. When she was old enough, she became a talker, smiled a lot, and loved to tag after Deborah and Simeon when they did their farm chores.

Nancy Ann was born in November of 1789. My Irish friends were in attendance at all the births, and so I was able to enjoy giving birth, almost, that is. Nancy Ann—we seemed to need to use both of her names—was a dear little baby girl. She had blue eyes, darker than her sisters' and brother's, but her eyes were very definitely blue. Hannah and Nancy exclaimed over yet another beautiful girl for us. As usual, Henry was not present at the birth of Nancy Ann, and did not have much interest in her as soon as he saw the color of her eyes! We saw him less often in those days, but he did return in the fall of 1891, when Simeon was just about to turn twenty, Deborah was a solemn nine, Hannah was a bouncy six year old, and Nancy Ann was toddling around at two.

That fall, when I was nearly fifty years old, I was able to remain cold to Henry longer than usual. The rumors of where he had been and what he had been doing were all over the nearby towns, and I was sick and tired of it all. Weaving and spinning and selling our goods amounted to a tiring job, and so were Henry's old and endless stories about why he had no money to help us. We lived simply, so he did not know that I had a small stash of savings well hidden away. As usual, he charmed me with his smiling eyes, played lovingly with his daughters, and one day he clapped Simeon on the shoulder and said, "You're man-grown now, son. Time you found a wife and settled down. Your mother is weary, and you need to begin to provide for her now."

That did not set well with either Sim or me. Both of us resented Henry's oh-so-free advice that he had never followed for himself. Neither of us made a reply to Henry, and when the till became empty, we knew he had left again. All of us, including Nancy, shared the relief that he was gone.

Simeon and I had often talked about Henry's power to charm me, and Sim begged me to resist it. Sim was often away in recent months, particularly when Henry was present. A childhood friend had re-entered Simeon's life. That friend's name was Richard Edgerly. Richard had the same ambition to settle new land that Sim had. Richard was nine years older than Sim and had worked for other people doing many different kinds of odd jobs. Richard had saved until he had enough money to buy some land in the "northern province of Massachusetts", as it was then called. Sim and Richard went to that area often in their travels, camped on the land they liked, and Simeon always returned more and more determined to live his dream. He thought of Richard as his older brother, and Sim listened to Richard's advice. Richard was a talented builder, and was a great help to Sim in planning his dreams.

Richard Edgerly was from a large and well-respected family, whose ancestors had helped settle Durham, N. H., in the 1600's. He was a younger son, and therefore did not think of inheriting any land from his father. In the early 1780's, he married Abigail Bickford, two years older than he. Richard was a large, handsome, brown haired man with the ruddy complexion of an outdoorsman. He loved to hunt and fish, and kept his own household and often ours too, supplied with meat and fish. Through all of the years that Abigail and I were friends, people thought we were sisters. However, neither of us could make that true. I was the only daughter of Benjamin Bickford. He was killed when I was twelve.

During the years I was giving birth to my four daughters, Abby was such a help and encouraged me " to hold a steady course." Our friendship continued to grow, as time went by. We remained fast friends all of our lives.

One day when he had just returned from what he was now calling "Gove's Ridge," Simeon said to me, "Please think about moving, Mom, I could build you the first home of your very own that you've ever had. Richard said he would help me design and build a home for you there."

Those were magic words, and he knew it! That winter, when my courses stopped, I had to face the fact that I was once more pregnant or else was I having my "change of life." As I was talking to myself and repeating my father's advice about dealing with difficulty: to straighten up my back, and ". .BE somebody," something happened that brought about a change in all our lives:

My belly was quite round, my feet swelled after a few hours at the loom, and I was out for a short walk in the early spring sunshine when a fancy painted wagon pulled up to the hitching post in front of our tailor shop. Henry jumped down from the wagon like a spry colt. The horse was a lively one, and the young girl in the wagon was dressed in satin and lace, but the fancy clothes didn't hide a belly somewhat bigger than mine. She had a very pretty, expensive bonnet on her head, too. Henry said, "Lydia, may I introduce Abigail Kenniston, from Durham. She and I are going on a short trip, and I would like to come in and pick up some of my things to take with us."

I thought of the till in the shop. My recent talk to myself was all the energy I needed that day. I drew myself up tall and shouted at him, "You are the Devil in person! There is nothing here for you. Take your doxy and begone from here. <u>DO NOT</u> come back, ever again!"

Having heard the noise outside, Simeon was standing in the open front door by then, with his rifle in plain sight.

"She means that, Sir, don't EVER come back."

"Well, I never heard such words and from my own family! Come, Dear Nabby, let's go!" Henry jumped back into his fancy wagon with his fancy young girl, and drove smartly away. I never expected to see him again, and I was not sorry. Just then, the baby kicked, and I knew for sure that I was not having the "change of life."

She was born on May 9, my fiftieth birthday. I named her Catherine. She was the smallest baby I ever delivered, and it was the hardest pregnancy and delivery that I ever had. Hannah and Nancy were very relieved and happy to announce a small but healthy baby girl once more. When I talked about names with them, the Irish girls said Catherine was a popular Saint in their religion, and that was my reason for her name. She really was a miracle baby. Neighbors were kind, and curious, too, I'm sure. After all, not many fifty year old women had babies those days. They came often to call, and brought gifts of food and things for the baby. They invited the older girls to visit for a few days in various homes, so I had some time to regain my strength. It seemed to take a very long time to come back, but eventually I was able to do the weaving, dyeing, and preparing of flax and wool to knit or weave. Mr. Remick's orders were as regular as ever, and so things settled, once more, into a routine at the Tufts Tailor Shop in Lee, N. H. My daily routine, because of my slow recovery, included an afternoon time of "quiet." Nancy was in charge of the house and shop during those times, and I was free to think about many things. Catherine was growing bigger and stronger, and feeding often and vigorously. Sim's words kept returning to my mind, and I did some "What iffing" as I relaxed in my rocking chair.

Young Thomas was getting to be man-grown, and Brother Thomas could well use the little cottage, I knew, for his son to begin life as an adult. Would he need the animals if we moved? Most important to my being able to earn a living, would Thomas need the tools in the Tailor Shop? I could always barter for nursing and/or birthing jobs, but would there be any such jobs in the wilderness? I wondered what Pa would do if he were in my shoes. I decided that I must have a talk with Brother Thomas, and maybe include Simeon in that talk, too.

The Irish girls were still knitting for shipment to Mr. Remick. Would they want to continue if I were not in Lee? And Mr. Remick: Who would make blankets for him? Could the Irish girls fill the gap that I might leave?

I decided that Pa would tell me to talk with the people who would be most affected if I left the tailor shop and Lee. I needed to have a lot of talks! I began with Hannah and Nancy. They were not surprised that I was thinking about going north with Sim. They were aware that Catherine's birth had taken its toll, and so they didn't seem shocked by my questions about the business with Portsmouth merchants. It was agreed that I would teach them my ways of making blankets, and they had enough money saved to buy a loom to share for making such fabric. They would like to continue the present method of knitting and selling sweaters, hats, scarves, and mittens for Mr. Remick, they said.

Simeon was glad to hear that my talks with the Irish girls turned out to be on the "go with Sim" side.

Next, I talked with Brother Thomas. His view on the animals, tools, and farm implements had not changed. He said, "Sim will need those things as he settles land, and so they are yours and his. As his need for different tools comes along, I will be glad to lend him some of mine. He will surely need some special tools that you probably don't have now. The tools for tailoring are yours, Lydia. The animals are all for you and Sim to share, too. If you have more animals than you can take with you, of course we'll care for them here. However, it's your decision which to take and which to leave."

Sim's face beamed with that speech. I could see plans forming in his head by the minute.

Thomas continued: "Please tell me how we can help you with all of this, Lydia. It will be a big move, but I think it will be a good one for you all. Your memories in this house can't be very pleasant for either of you, and I think you'll prosper better somewhere new. Also, the neighbors still talk about 'Crazy Mary' and the mean things she did. That, I know."

It was hard for me to speak for a few minutes, but finally I got a voice to say, "Thank you, Thomas, I don't know what I would do without your kindness."

"Lydia, you have paid for any kindnesses in advance. You made a great difference to my parents' final years, and your patience with Henry has not gone unnoticed. We can't really make up for the problems he's caused you, but you have been patient through it all. I must add that both Liz and I were glad to hear that he'll not be bothering you any more."

It was now time for me and Sim to talk "turkey," as the expression went. The day after we had talked with Thomas, Simeon and I discussed money. The money I had hidden away was a surprise to him, and his eyes filled up a bit when I asked him how much he needed to purchase some land on Gove's Ridge. He told me that he had his eyes on a hundred acres of high ridge land that he thought could be cleared and used for a good farm. It was located near an old

Indian Trail called the Sokokis Trail. Apparently, Indians still used the Trail to go to their spring fishing grounds out of the White Mountains to the north and west. He said that Mr. Gove called them "peaceful Indians."

Simeon told me how much money he had and how much he needed to buy his treasured one hundred acres. We shook hands and agreed to buy the land.

Chapter 15

1792 – 1793
Moving

As Catherine grew, she remained small in size for her age. As a tiny toddler, she developed a set of likes and dislikes that she made known to us all. She did not like loud noises. When she cried at an unexpected loud voice, I was reminded of her first signal to me that she would join us in this world—a kick when I yelled at Henry.

During that fall of 1792, Simeon was the happiest I had ever seen him. When he was leaving for Gove's Ridge to buy his land and I handed him my share of the money, I watched him skip a step or two like a child as he went to mount his horse. When he returned, he told me that he and Richard had thought they would buy land located in a place called "The Ossipee Plantation," an Indian name. However, the land they were interested in settling, that same land, was now located in the newly formed Town of Limington, in the " Northern Province of Mayne."

That fall and winter were full of plans and more plans. With Richard's help, Sim drew up plans for my cabin. I needed room for my four girls to sleep, eat, do their learning from chapbooks, and live; we needed to provide for plenty of heat in the north country; we needed to provide for a few animals—cows and goats for milk and cheeses, pig for meat, sheep for wool and meat; hens for eggs and stews, and so on. I wanted my cabin to face toward the south with its back to the north wind, and I wanted a fireplace large enough to heat the cabin as well as to cook our food. I needed room for the Barn Loom, the Walking wheel, and the other tailoring tools. With Richard's help, Sim bent over the cutting table in the tailor shop for many hours planning and drawing. As they worked, Abby and I enjoyed my girls and talked and talked.

The girls grew used to the news of the coming move, each in her own way:

Deborah asked serious questions: "Momma, how are we going to get to Gove's Ridge? Will it take a long time? What will we take with us? Where is Gove's Ridge, anyway?"

Hannah told everyone she knew, "We're moving to the wilderness! Won't that be fun?"

Nancy Ann quietly smiled and said little. Catherine listened to all the talk with big, round, blue and somewhat worried eyes beneath her blonde curly top.

My dear Irish girls, Hannah and Nancy, took over more and more of the work in the shop. They were making plans of their own to rent a small cottage where they could live and work together to continue to supply knitted goods and woven blankets to the Portsmouth merchants. They talked of forming a "cottage industry" such as they had seen in Ireland, in which they would teach other knitters to make Aran knits with their directions and with the yarn they provided. They would pay the other knitters a few pence for their work, and then re-sell the items to Mr. Remick. It seemed like a good idea to me.

I sent Mr. Remick a letter telling him of my plans, and suggesting that he begin to deal with the Irish girls directly, as they could supply him with all that he needed in the future. I thanked him, too, for his years of fair business dealings with me.

There was not time for Simeon to visit Thomas in Northwood in early spring of 1793. He was too busy making trips to Gove's Ridge to work on my cabin. Thomas brought young Thomas to Lee to see the little cottage for himself. Young Thomas was like Brother Thomas—quiet, thoughtful, tall, with dark hair, and snapping dark brown eyes. I didn't test to see if he smiled with his eyes. I didn't want to know.

It was a pleasant visit, and the two Thomases made some plans for their use of the little Tufts cottage. The Tailor Shop sign and the hitching posts would be taken down, and several other changes would make the little cottage belong to its new owner. I was glad to see they were making such plans, because our departure date had been set: we would leave Lee forever on my fifty first birthday, May 9, 1793. Catherine would be one year old, and Sim would be twenty two and a half. I said a prayer of thanks as Catherine struggled to walk around the time for her first birthday.

Before I knew it, I was weaving my last blanket on the Barn Loom in the Tufts cottage. It was a bittersweet experience. By 1793, the wood on the old loom had some "use spots" where the old buttermilk red paint had been worn thin or completely off by Lydia Bickford Tufts, I thought. However, I knew that I would weave other fabrics on it in another place. All was not over.

When the last blanket to be sent to Mr. Remick was ready, I made the trip to Capt. Follett's with Old Kit, by myself with my girls, to deliver my last shipment for Portsmouth and to say Goodbye and thanks to Capt. Follett for his kindnesses through the years. The Capt. wished us all well and admired my girls,

"They are all so pretty, Lydia, and look so much like you! I know that this move will do you all good, and I know your Simeon well enough to know he is a good man and he will care for you all and keep you safe. Godspeed!"

Our neighbors had planned an old fashioned Frolic to send us off. It was to be held in the Tufts barn. The Irish girls were included in the planning, and so our fireplaces were laden with pot luck dishes on the day of the gathering. Anyone who could play an instrument was invited to do so, and we had a merry old fashioned time. It was as well that it happened a week before we were to start our trip, because we all needed a few days to bring ourselves back to earth from all of the gifts, good wishes, hugs and kisses, dancing, and funny stories of happenings since Simeon and I had moved in with Pa and Mary Tufts in 1772. Twenty two years of funny stories took all afternoon and evening, mixed in with the dancing and the eating, and gave us good memories to last a long time. I was glad it was not a husking bee, as I could not have made it through that kind of frolic without Henry. As it was, I remembered him only once or twice during the evening, and I noticed the stories were carefully told without his name in them.

Two days before we were to start, the loom was taken apart, the pieces carefully labeled, and then loaded in the bottom of one of the wagons we were to take. Thus the move began. The spinning wheel was more delicate, and so it was left to put on top of my load. Richard and Sim had asked for a "family meeting" in which they would explain the things that were going to happen, give each of us a job to do on the trip, and answer any thing the little girls wondered about.

Each of us would have a heavy blanket, a pillow and a light blanket to sleep with at night. They were our "bedrolls." Each of the girls was to care for her own bedroll. We would make a camp each night, and Simeon and Richard had planned the places where we would stop to rest along the way. They hoped that the trip would take about a week in all. As they described the way we would do things, the trip seemed to be something that we could, with our ages spread from one to fifty-one, do all right.

Sim's old Laddie, now with some white fur around his muzzle, was very much a part of the activities at the Tufts place. During the busy days of getting ready for the move, Laddie himself was on the move keeping track of four girls, five adults, and all the animals. When he found something or someone doing something strange, or standing in a strange place, he made a single "Woof" and tried to nudge, using his long, cold nose, the out-of-place person or animal into Laddie's idea of the right place.

On our departure day, when everything was loaded and all the animals were in their places, Sim called Laddie and lifted his tired old body onto Sim's wagon and said,

"Now, Laddie, you stay there. Everything is fine. Just stay!"

We made quite a long string that must have looked like a funny parade: First, Richard led the way driving a team of oxen. He called his oxen "Star" and "Line." They would set the pace for all of us. The oxen were hitched to a wagon Richard had made from thick planks. It was long and deep, with high sides and big heavy wheels that had iron rims on them. Richard knew how to shape metal as well as any blacksmith, and he had done a sturdy job with all of our wagon wheels. We would have several streams and rivers to ford, he had explained, and they must be big and sturdy. Richard's wagon was loaded with all of the bedrolls, the camping/cooking/eating things, and spare clothes for the children. On top of this load, Abby sat like a queen, holding the hands of their eight year old Samuel and their one year old Jacob. Tied to the back of that wagon were three sheep and a cow.

Second, Simeon drove Prince pulling an old buckboard loaded with hay for the animals, all of the furniture that he had not made in place on Gove's Ridge, a coop with hens that would lay eggs for us to eat on the trip, and a box with a small piglet in it. Hitched to the back of Sim's wagon were two more cows and two goats. Riding with him were Deborah and Hannah, each in her new "poke bonnet" that would keep the sun away. Like Richard's wagon, Sim's had large wheels and set high off the road to keep the contents of the wagons dry when we had to ford rivers.

I was third in line, driving Old Kit with the buckboard we had taken to Northwood in such haste years before. Nancy Ann and Catherine were beside me in their new poke bonnets, and there was a pillow under our seat for Catherine to use when she got tired. Our wagon had all of my tailoring tools as well as extra clothes for the adults and more hay for the animals. Hitched to the back of my wagon were another cow and two more sheep. Like the other wagons, Richard had made wheels for my buckboard that were large and made for the girls and me a good climb to get up into and down away from the wagon whenever we stopped.

Last of all came a small wagon, pulled by a single ox that was driven by a young man named Seth. Simeon had hired him to help on the trip. That wagon was loaded with two crates of pigs and shoats, more chickens, more hay, and hitched to the back of that wagon was the bull with a ring in his nose. Like the others, the wagon had very large wheels and set high off the road.

Our neighbors all were outside to wave us a last farewell. After all of the planning and loading and hoping for the future, it was good to be off on the traveling part of our journey. The New Hampshire roads were wide enough to allow two wagons to meet and pass each other. We were to keep in single file in case we met another wagon coming toward us. If a message was needed between our wagons, Deborah or Hannah or Richard's Samuel could run fast enough to deliver it. The roads were flat and free of large boulders, so the wagons rolled along well. Before we left Lee, I forded a river for the first time.

The Lamprey River, I had always said, "eeled" its way through Lee into Great Bay, turning this way and that like an eel because the land it flows over is so flat. We must have crossed it seven times on our way north and east to Durham. Sim and Richard had planned our first camping spot in Durham, just before we would need to ford the Oyster River there. We were all glad to hear the call to "Halt!" The older girls and I were a bit disappointed that we had traveled only five miles that first day. However, we had started late because of last minute packing of wagons and hitching up of animals, and so, as Sim said,

"Five miles is better than none."

We stopped in daylight for that night, because those of us who were going to Gove's Ridge for the first time needed to learn how to make camp quickly. First, while the rest of us came to a halt and watched and waited, Richard guided his oxen into the large, open area that was to be our resting place. It surrounded a firepit. There was no fire, so he guided his oxen to pull the wagon close to the firepit where it would be parked for the night. The wagon was placed near enough to the firepit so the contents were handy for cooking and eating our meal. Then he unhitched Star and Line and took them to the area where he could remove their yoke and give them feed and water. He tied them to hitching posts there, where they would spend the night. Meanwhile, we unloaded the cooking and eating things and Abby and I began to get our evening meal, which we had cooked in Lee the day before. Deborah helped the younger girls spread out the bedrolls in the area Sim had shown her. A wooden bowl and carved spoon for each person, gifts from our friends, were taken out and set around the fire. Deborah showed the other girls how to put out their bedrolls. Catherine's would be nearest mine, of course.

After Richard's wagon was placed, it was Sim's turn. He pulled Prince in beside Richard's wagon and at a slight angle so it looked like we were beginning a fan of wagons. He unhitched the horse and led him away to be unharnessed and watered and fed. The tethering spot was in sight of the campfire, and it was close to a small stream for watering all the animals. Each wagon carried a pail with a long handled cup in it for drinking during the long days. Those pails were used to carry water to all of the animals morning and night.

The hens in the crates had produced five eggs, only one of which had broken, so there were eggs enough to make the cornbread. I pulled Kit in beside Sim's wagon at an angle, as he had done. I led Kit toward her friend, Prince, for her night feeding. Sim took her to unharness and settle with food and water for the night. Next came Seth, who repeated the action that he had seen the others do. After taking his ox to be tethered, he watered and fed the animals hitched to the backs of the wagons, and loosened their tie-ups so they could lie down. They seemed relieved to eat and drink and have a chance to lie down. Laddie "supervised" it all, and when he seemed satisfied that all was well, he went to Sim's side and lay down.

As soon as Richard was finished feeding and watering animals, he built the fire, so Abby and I could warm our supper and bake the cornbread. With the wagons placed fan-like around one side of the firepit, we had the opposite side for eating and then sleeping. All the bedrolls were laid out, with the children nearer the fire and the adults in a semi-circle outside the children. Before long, with animals all chewing contentedly, we sat down with our supper.

As we ate, sitting in a semi-circle on our side of the glowing fire, Sim said,

"Well, family, tonight's settling in was a bit slow. We need to get our jobs well in mind so that we can do it faster. I'm sure it will come with practice. Just think of the jobs we need to do, rain or shine, whenever we settle down for the night. First, the animals must be fed and watered, then we ourselves can settle down. In the mornings, we will all do the same jobs in reverse. Deborah, you will see that all the bedrolls are carefully rolled up and loaded onto Richard's wagon." He went down the list of jobs and who would do each one.

Abby and I cleaned up the wooden bowls and spoons as well as the cooking dishes with water that had been heating over the fire. Deborah settled the girls down in their bedrolls for the night.

It was not long before snores were replacing the small-talk of bedtime. I gazed up to the stars as bright as diamonds in the sky, and thanked my God for a pleasant day with interesting new things to learn. Sim and Richard must have been very tired. They had explained to all of us how to do what we needed to do for the entire day. I knew that Sim was not a man of words, and neither was Richard.

The following day, we reversed the process of feeding and watering animals, eating, and then loading the wagons. We knew that this day would be longer than the day before. I made sure that each girl had her doll and her chapbook with her before we set out. Traveling slowly would wear on them, and they needed things to keep their minds busy. Simeon reminded us about making sure that all hot coals and ashes from our cook fire were put out before we left the campsite. Deborah was appointed the one who would get a bucket of water from the brook and douse the ashes well.

"We are not the only people who need places to stop on a long trip," he told us, "and we must leave things for other travelers, who will be as tired as we were when they get here."

Through Durham, the roads were very wide and smooth, so we made good time. Fording the Oyster River was different than fording the Lamprey. It was deeper, and the sheep and goats needed to be carried across on a ferry. The horses, oxen, and cows had legs long enough to wade the River, but the sheep and goats hitched to the backs of the wagons had shorter legs needed a boat to get cross. As we waited for the ferry, Sim told the girls about ferries,

"We'll need more ferry rides to cross two more big rivers before we get to Berwick in the "northern territory of Mayne." We'll cross the Cocheeco River in Dover and the Salmon Falls River when we go between New Hampshire and into Berwick in the wilderness territory of 'Mayne.' After that, we'll go through Waterboro and then we'll have many miles of travel in the sandy pine woods, with tall pine trees all around, to our new home on Gove's Ridge in Limington."

All of the girls were interested, and they reacted to Sim's talk in their usual ways. Deborah gravely, Hannah joyously, Nancy Ann with a small smile, and Catherine with her big eyes looking at him silently. All of my girls loved their big, strong, brother and tried to please him in every way they could. Richard and Abby and Seth listened to Sim's talk, too, quietly and with Richard and Abby's heads nodding up and down. Abby had been to Gove's Ridge once, and she was excited to be going there to live, I knew. Her happiness about our move helped my girls and me face the unknown without fear of the many new things we were sure to meet in this move.

After what seemed like a very long delay, the ferryman arrived on our side of the Oyster River, and the sheep and goats were loaded into a pen on his ferry. He showed Richard and Sim the best route to take the horses and oxen across the River. Sim tied Prince to a tree, and helped to load all of the small animals onto the ferry while Richard drove his oxen to lead me and Seth across the River. When they arrived, we tied up the sheep and goats on the far side of the River, and Sim then returned on the ferry to drive Prince and his wagon across to join us. Meanwhile, Richard and Seth had the small animals tied to their respective wagons once more.

Lesson learned: Rivers are a big challenge to travel, but, like other things, given the time and careful planning, there is a safe way to overcome!

Sim talked to the ferryman about camping places we might find on our way to Dover. He mentioned one about a mile on our way. Richard and Sim decided that one more hour would be a good day's trip for us, and so we set off toward the Dover rest stop.

When we reached the camping spot, we realized we were all very tired. Everyone had worked hard that day, and so a light supper seemed in order. While the men fed and watered the animals, Abby and I got ready to serve warmed-over hotch-potch and warmed-over cornbread that night, promising a good hearty breakfast of bacon, eggs, and biscuits baked over the fire the next morning. The hens were producing plenty of eggs, so we were feeling glad about that. Many times, a change in routine would make hens stop laying eggs, but those biddies were not to be deterred!

Abby and I were up early the next morning to prepare a big breakfast for what promised to be a long day ahead. It was our third day on the trip and it was very much like day number two had been. After the morning routine, we traveled only a short way until we reached the Cocheeco River in the Town of Dover, New Hampshire. There, we repeated the pattern set at the Oyster River in Durham. We needed a ferry to get the small animals that were not in cages on the wagons across the Cocheeco River. That night, we camped in sight of our goal—Berwick, Mayne was just across the last and widest River we needed to cross. The girls were very excited, but fell asleep quickly after the busy day. That night I said a thank you prayer for the good weather we'd had up until then. I prayed it would continue for just a few more days until we reached our goal. The bright stars again shone down and promised a good day tomorrow.

Day number four repeated the routine that we all seemed to be comfortable with by this time. Even the animals, including our dear Laddie, acted used to the routine of watering, eating, and resting that had been set for them. The ferryman to help us cross the Salmon Falls River— the biggest one yet—was known to Sim, who called him "Mr. Stone." Sim had been to Gove's Ridge often, and he had shared our coming move with Mr. Stone. As soon as we were all on the far side of the River, Mr. Stone said,

"She's waiting for you, Sim. She ain't been fit to live with for days!"

Sim just smiled, and Richard winked at me.

We formed up our parade and headed into pine woods on the sandy road. After less than a mile, Richard stopped the oxen and Sim pulled far over to the side of the road to stop. I stopped Kit the same way, and Seth pulled up his ox and cart behind me.

There stood the prettiest girl I had seen for a very long time. She seemed to be about eighteen, with bobbing brown curls and smiling hazel eyes. She was hopping up and down, first on one foot and then on the other, waving her hands, and smiling as though she saw something very special coming her way. Sim jumped down from his seat, grabbed her around the waist, and gave her a resounding kiss. He brought her to my wagon, and said,

"Mother, I would like you to meet the girl I am going to marry as soon as I can. Her name is Elizabeth Stone, and I call her 'Lib.'"

What to say? 'Stone' rang a bell—she was the ferryman's daughter, of course! I reached down for her hand,

"I'm so glad to meet you, Lib, and I look forward to many happy years on Gove's Ridge with you as part of our family. Will you come with us now?"

"No, Mother Tufts, I cannot come with you now. My mother is very sick and I need to take care of her for a few more months. I hope you understand."

I did, and I liked what I heard about her sense of duty. I introduced her to my girls, and each of them gave her a shy smile. Thus, we met a person who would be an important part of our new life on Gove's Ridge.

Chapter 16

1793
Gove's Ridge

The little girls' questions came to me in a gaggle: Nancy Ann: "Will she be our sister?" Catherine: "Lib, Lib?"

Nancy Ann: "Will she live with us in our new house?"

I smiled at the thought of the questions that were going on in Sim's wagon as soon as he had said his goodbye to Lib and climbed up to his seat. All the girls liked Lib, I knew, and so Sim should be happy. I liked what I knew of his choice, and I looked forward to getting to know her better.

As we went along under the tall pine trees, I became aware of the sandy road the oxen and horses were pulling us over. The wagons did not roll along as well as they had in New Hampshire on the more traveled hard roads. The wheels sank down into the sand so as to nearly cover the wooden rims. It was much harder and slower going for the animals after we had arrived in the Northern Province.

Something was missing, I decided, when I sniffed but could no longer smell salt air or when I listened and could not hear waves breaking on the shore. Funny, I had not missed it until we were this far into our new life. The sound of breakers, I decided, was replaced by the soft whisper of the wind in the pines, and the smell of salt air was replaced by the tang of the pines as they moved in the wind and as we drove over the needles that had dropped to the ground. New sounds and new smells were not bad, just different. I must be ready to answer questions about that from the older girls, I thought.

As we moved along, sleepy Catherine began a nap on her pillow and Nancy Ann at last had asked everything about Sim and Lib that she could think of. She put her tired little head in my lap and fell asleep, too. I was left to my thoughts. It was time for a little "What-iffing" for me.

It would be nice if I could share the surprise of meeting the girl Sim intended to marry with Henry—and if Henry could be interested. It made me sad, when I thought of it, that Henry did not choose to share much of anything of his life, and none of his family's lives and thoughts. Soon I told myself to stop the bad thoughts and to be grateful to have a grown-up son and four healthy, happy, girls, all with different ways of doing things and ways of looking at the world.

Keeping Kit's head aimed straight ahead and away from nibbling anything and everything beside the trail kept me from falling into a doze.

I did not dare to doze, because I knew what her nibbles brought about—severe colic that needed all-night care.

As we moved along the sandy trail—it was not a road anymore, I decided—we moved more and more slowly. It was very hard work for the oxen and horses to pull our heavy wagons and the loads the wagons carried through the ever deepening sand.

We crossed a small brook that ran from our left to our right where it tumbled over noisy rapids into a river on our right. Later, Sim told me that was the Great Works River. Shortly after we crossed the brook, I looked up to see yet another challenge for our animals. It was a hill of sand! Out loud I said, "How will we ever get up that great hill?" As soon as the words were out, we got the signal "Halt." Nancy Ann sat up and Catherine turned over on her pillow.

Sim came to my wagon and said, "This is the hardest part of our whole trip. We'll take this hill slow. We'll rest here before we begin it, then we'll go up one at a time. Richard will go first, hitch his oxen and he'll come back to lead Prince. Then I'll come back to lead Kit and he'll take Seth's ox up the hill. We'll stop about a third of the way up and again about another third of the way. After we all get over the hilltop, there's a good place to camp for tonight just down into a small swale. There's a good spring there for water, too."

Richard started out with his team of strong oxen. They moved very slowly, but they did not stop until they were about a third of the way up, as Sim had told us. Although it took a long time, all went as planned, and at long last we all were over the top and down into the cool glade that Sim had called a "swale." I wondered if that was a local word. I had never heard it before.

We were very glad, all of us, to stop for the night. With the excitement of Sim's news about Lib, as well as the new sights, sounds, smells, and hills, too, I was weary on this night number four.

It was a good campsite. The spring bubbled out of the ground cool and good-tasting. After the animals were tended, Abby and I had a tasty hotchpotch of bacon, potatoes, carrots, and turnip plus some wild onions that were growing near the spring. Everyone seemed to enjoy the meal with the cornbread that was hot from the iron spider that night. During the evening chat, Richard and Sim seemed to think that two more nights on the road were the most we would need to reach the Ridge. That was good news to me. I was getting tired of sleeping on the ground, and I yearned for a featherbed to rest my weary bones.

Next morning, to begin day five, Abby and I made bacon, eggs, and biscuits once more. They were well received. Soon, we must remember to put some oats on the fire to cook all night, but last night we had not remembered to do so. Too tired.

There was more slow going in the soft sand on day five. The animals seemed to have adjusted, and seemed to make more headway that day. We began to see small ponds by the sides of the trail, and Sim said we were in the Town of Waterborough, named for the many lakes and ponds in it. We would remain in Waterborough, on sandy trails and among the pine trees, until we crossed the Little Ossippee River and climbed onto Gove's Ridge itself, he told us. The bright sun was beginning to make the girls glad for their poke bonnets, as it was hot and shone steadily all day. That day brought new sights and smells. All around us in the sand were blueberry bushes in blossom. It looked as though there would be a big crop. I made a vow to return, if this area was not too far from Gove's Ridge, for picking blueberries come July or August. The new smell was sweet and spicy. I noticed a low shrub with branches of tiny leaves shaped like a fern on it. When I was near one on the ground, I picked it and crushed it in my hand. That was the new smell, and I asked Abby what it could be. She did not know and neither did the men. We named it ourselves: it was to be called "Sweet Fern."

The campsite for our stop on day five was at a lakeside. No one seemed to know the name of the lake, there were so many in the Town of Waterborough. That night we took the animals down to the lake to get their drinks of water. They seemed to like that, and after the long, sandy day, they drank deeply and waded around in the water.

That night, Abby and I remembered to put the oats on the fire for our breakfast, and so we had bowls of hot oatmeal to eat the next morning. The cows had been milked twice each day, and we had cottage cheese as well as cream on our oatmeal that morning.

Day six dawned cloudy, and we all crossed fingers that we could get to the shelter of my cabin for that night. We ate our breakfast as fast as possible, and were soon hitched up all around and on our usual way, with Richard leading, Sim, me, and Seth to bring up the rear.

After what seemed like only a few miles, I noticed that the sandy trails were becoming harder and easier for the animals, the pine trees were farther back from our trail, and we had a river on our right. The blueberry bushes and "Sweet Fern" remained beside the trail along our way. The river was shallow, but very rocky and full of large boulders that looked to have been thrown there, hit or miss, by a giant.

Sim called a halt, and gathered us for a talk. "We are very near our last fording. Richard and I cleared the River bed—the "Little Ossippee"— for our crossing. Just to be sure, he will cross, hitch his oxen, then come back to lead Prince around any new boulders that may be there. As soon as Prince is safely across, I'll hitch him to a tree and come back for Ma and Kit. Please don't anyone who has not crossed this river before try it without someone to lead your animal. That would be dangerous. When we are all across, then we'll follow Richard up to the top of Gove's Ridge and be home in Limington!"

I said a short thank you prayer for my wise and careful son, his friend Richard, and our safe and nearly completed journey. Capt. Follett was right—Sim was careful for our safety, and had taken much on his young shoulders to get us all here safely.

The climb up to the top of Gove's Ridge was quite steep, but it was over ledge and solid earth, not sand. Pine trees lingered all around though, and their smell along with the Sweet Fern would be always with us, I thought. I rather liked that.

Soon, our parade was climbing up to the top of the Ridge. In back of us was the River, on the horizon far back of us was a small cone of a hill that sparkled even in the dull light of a cloudy day. To our left and north were the layers of the White Mountains on the horizon and nearby the land sloped down and off the Ridge. To our right and south the land sloped more gradually down to the tree line, marking where the clearing of the land had stopped. We passed a small set of buildings that were made up of a house and barn and climbed a small rise to see a newly built log cabin that set exactly on the highest point of land on the Ridge. The logs had been squared off and presented flat sides to the world—later, they could be painted or left to weather into shades of gray.

"Welcome, Mother Tufts, to your new home." the adults all said together.

I couldn't speak. It was perfect. There was a small fenced-in area for the sheep and goats, tie-ups for the cows, horses and oxen, and even a separate place to put the bull!

Simeon said, "It isn't finished, Mother, but it will be before long. I hope you will like it and have a long and happy life here in your own 'wilderness.'"

My girls were hopping up and down with excitement, and sensible Deb said, "Well. Mom, are you going to look inside?"

I climbed down from my wagon and lifted Nancy Ann and Catherine down, too. We all went into our new home. The inside was as perfect as the outside. This is what greeted us: First, we climbed up a few steps to a wide porch. The new wood smell was fresh and a little sweet—like the pine wood it had been made from. There was room for at least two rocking chairs on the porch, I noticed. We opened the door into the cabin and came into more and stronger smells of new pine wood. Over our heads, in the high part of the one-pitch roof, was the sleeping loft, complete with a ladder to reach it on the right. Looking down the right wall, I saw a small window facing west. Pieces of mica, or "isenglass," had been fitted into the frame to let in the daylight. Under the window and for the full length of the west wall were several single bunk bed frames, ready to be filled with feather beds and blankets that could be used for sitting or for sleeping. Most of the back wall, which, I decided quickly, faced north because it was without windows, held a massive native rock fireplace. On the right side of the fireplace, there was room for a double bunk. "Mine," I thought. Left of the fireplace was more space where I could imagine a settle, a built-in closet, a table with 6 chairs, and across the corner could be another floor to ceiling closet. Further to the right, the east wall held one door. I looked quickly to see that the sleeping loft would allow my barn loom to fit under it, and there was room for my walking wheel, too, just to the right of the door to the porch. The table, when it was finished, would allow cutting out of garments as well as eating and getting meals, and the walls would hold all of the pegs I might want for drying hanks of yarn and yards of cloth. Like the outside, it was perfect!

How Simeon had done all of this in the times he had been here, I did not know. Richard had been building his own cabin just north of mine, and Sim had done some work on his cabin north of Richard and Abby's.

Sim, Abby and Richard, and Seth crowded through the front door to see how I liked it all. I had tears rolling down my cheeks; I could not stop them. This was my first real home, and it was just what I had dreamed about. Sim had listened to my wishes so well that he had made my dreams come true! Could anyone ask for more?

"It's not finished, mother," Sim said a little sadly, "I had hoped to have it all done, but I couldn't."

"No matter, Sim," I replied, "It is my dream home already. I love it!"

Chapter 17

1793 ~ 1794

Before anyone asked them to do so, the older girls began to unload their bedrolls and put them in their new home. The two older girls would sleep in the loft, and Nancy Ann and Catherine would sleep on the main floor—Catherine was to sleep with me until she was comfortable in a single bunk bed of her own. For their first night, though, they would unroll their bedrolls onto the wood boards of the first floor. In time, we would install their featherbeds into their proper places.

Everyone was hungry, so the men built a fire in the new fireplace and we began to get our first meal on Gove's Ridge, Limington, ready to eat. I wanted something special, so Sim suggested that we roast little pig, who had traveled to his destiny in style in the back of a wagon all the way from Lee, New Hampshire. Sim lit the first fire I saw in my new fireplace. It did not smoke once; the chimney drew perfectly. The smoke went up the chimney and out into the crisp air of early May.

I discovered this was no ordinary fireplace. It had a special spit to roast meat, and when the men brought the pork inside to be roasted, it was put on the spit. The pork was cooked and ready to eat in a short time and while that was going on, Abby and I prepared some of our vegetables in an iron pot that hung from one of the several built-in cranes with its trummel to adjust the distance the pot hung from the fire.

The older Edgerly boys, Samuel at eight, and Jacob at one, would need some teaching from chapbooks before long, along with my older girls, so I could see in my mind a little school in my cabin some day.

The little cabin buzzed with activity as the girls began to put their possessions in special places. Deborah's doll was made of porcelain, so she had to be handled carefully and placed in safe places. Serious Deb was a perfect doll mother. The other girls had wooden dolls, but they were careful with them, too. We found an area to hang their chapbooks where they could reach them when it was time to study. For their arithmetic, I would have to make up problems—there would be no change to make for customers in the tailor shop to teach the girls and boys how to subtract. I must find a purpose for them to learn arithmetic, or else they wouldn't try to learn it, I knew. The tailor shop had been a perfect place to teach Simeon, but we would find something on Gove's Ridge, I knew.

It was soon time to find seats for everyone to sit with his or her bowl and eat the supper that smelled so good. Sim and Richard and Seth brought in large chunks of trees and stood them on end for us adults to use as seats. As we ate, we chatted about how the night would be spent. The animals had all been watered and fed, and were tethered or fenced safely for the night. The wagon contents had been covered in case it rained. Seth and Sim would walk the Ridge west to Sim's cabin, where there was shelter waiting for them. Richard, Abby, and their two boys would sleep with us in my new cabin, in case any of us new to the wilderness heard unfamiliar noises.

The boys and Richard and Abby would go up the ladder to the sleeping loft. My older girls decided they would like to remain on the first floor near Catherine and me for that first night. Richard and Sim had checked the land around my cabin for tracks, and found none. However, I knew, even though I did not share it with my girls, that bear, wolves, foxes, panthers, and other wild animals were our near neighbors now. Not to frighten my girls, I left the complete list of wild animals we would now live with unsaid, but I did forbid leaving our porch after dark, and for many weeks, I made sure my girls obeyed that rule.

Unpacking the wagons and getting accustomed to our new surroundings took several days, which turned into weeks, and soon it was time for Sim to take Seth to his home in Lee. They would take Prince and the buckboard and Sim would bring back another load of hay for our animals on the Ridge. Sim would also bring his horse, Sally, to the Ridge. She was a fast little saddle horse, and could take him to visit his "Lib" faster than Prince could, at his age, make the trip.

The "boys" set off in the buckboard early one morning, and the girls and I were beginning to know our surroundings well enough to feel more at home on Gove's Ridge. Sim had taken us to meet the Gove brothers, our nearest neighbors across the Sokokis Trail. Sim and Richard trusted the Goves, and asked them many questions. In one of the talks we all had, I learned that Sim's holdings of 100 acres was north and west of Richard's. My cabin was built on Richard's land, because Sim wanted it to be on the highest point of land with a view in all of the directions of the compass—north, south, east, and west. When I no longer could use it, the cottage would go back to Richard's ownership. That was the law in those days, and so I accepted it all, with thanks to Richard for allowing me to live out my life in my very own cabin, no matter on whose land it was built.

The Goves lived in the small set of buildings we had seen as we began to climb onto the Ridge that first day. They were not there very much, having larger homes in Portland. They still had large holdings of land in the area, and came to the Ridge only when dealing with the management of it.

Before long, Sim was home once more. He had brought his "Sally," as well as a good wagonload of hay for our animals. It was getting to be time to mow the small patches of grains and hay that he and Richard had found time to sow in early spring. We could eke out enough for the animals during the coming winter, but it would be a narrow eke. My girls enjoyed playing in their new surroundings, and Samuel was a good teacher about where to find berries, flowers, and other treasures of nature on the Ridge.

Sam would jump onto our front porch yelling, "C'mon, girls, get your buckets! Strawberries are ripe!" Later it was "Blueberries are ripe! Get your buckets, girls." In September, it was "Elderberries are ripe! C'mon, girls get your buckets!" The rest of the fall until snow fell, he would yell, "Butt'nuts are ready!"

The Edgerley's house was just to the north, and it was growing into a handsome two story Garrison house with an ell at the back that held the kitchen. The end of the kitchen that faced northeast was made up entirely of a fireplace bigger than mine, and I can still remember the smell of roasting pork on the spit in that house as well as in mine. Richard was the stone mason who had built both fireplaces, and he had done two fine jobs.

Sim's visits to Lib were more frequent now, and in the fall of 1793, he told us that Lib's mother was failing, and might not live through the winter. That meant that we would have a wedding sometime during 1794. Meanwhile, Sim worked on my cabin to put the finishing touches onto it, like rocking chairs for the front porch, a large table and six chairs for the east side of my cabin, corner cupboards and bunk beds, as well as beds in the sleeping loft. My barn loom was set up, a flax pond appeared, all lined with clean rocks for soaking the flax I would grow in another year, and so on.

My serious Deborah said, "Mom, Sim is building you a mansion!"

"You are just right, Deborah, and I can't wait to teach you all about how to use all of these things. You're nearly big enough to weave now, and I think some lessons will soon be in order. You have picked enough berries for this year!"

Hannah, in her happy way, wanted to learn about everything, too. Each girl learned to spin, to weave, to knit, and to sew. Soon, they were always busy doing one of the fiber tasks. I did not allow either one to use the hackles much during the fall and winter of 1794, when we had our first crop of flax on the Ridge, but they observed how it is treated, at least.

All four girls had their chapbook lessons as well as their fiber lessons. They seemed to do well in reading and writing, but arithmetic was a conundrum. How could I make it a necessary thing to know their times tables, subtraction and addition? I pondered that for quite a while, then one day Sam came up with an idea: "Mrs. T, how about we measure in our berry pails and then see how many pails full it will take to make a gallon?"

We began by measuring water, then we went to grain, and so on. Soon, Sam and the girls were measuring fabric to estimate how much it would take to make Sim's wedding shirt. During early fall in 1794, there was much excitement on Gove's Ridge. Sim and Lib set their wedding date.

Two events were to take place in 1794, and both events took place in Berwick. They happened this way: During April of 1794, I finished examining Abby, who was very pregnant.

"Abby, I hate to tell you this, but your baby is due soon. It's now mid-April, and by this time next month, I think the baby will be here. However, unless I miss my guess, he will want to come into the world breach. That means, fanny first, and I do not have the people or the tools to help you with a breach birth here on the Ridge. I wish you would go to Berwick with Sim next week and let a doctor examine you. He might be able to turn the baby, or else to help you with a breach birth, in ways that I can't."

It was hard for me to tell her that, but I could not endanger her life or the baby's by being too confident and by taking risks.

"Thank you, Lydia, I'll talk about it with Richard. I think he'll agree to take me to a Dr., and maybe Lib will know of one in Berwick who can help me."

I spoke with Richard, too, and it was arranged that Abby and Richard would go with Sim the next time he went to see his Lib and they would see a doctor in Berwick. So it happened that young Isaac Edgerly joined his parents in Berwick on May 15, 1794. That made three boys for Richard and Abby. When Abby arrived home in June, we had good laughs over their trying to compete with my four girls. While they were gone, Sam and Jacob stayed with my girls and me. While Abby was recovering in Berwick, Richard came home to tell his boys about their little brother, as well as to tend to his animals.

The usual farm seasonal jobs were on-going. Isaac joined his family during planting season. Then, for Sam and the girls, it was strawberrying season, and on it went. Sim and Lib planned their wedding to be held after the fall harvest was in. They were married by a Justice of the Peace in Berwick on November 7, 1794. Sim was my pride and joy as he set off in the buckboard with Prince. My girls had decorated both the horse and the old wagon with green boughs of fir and Sweet Fern. Sim wore the linsey-woolsey shirt I had woven and made for him. His pants were the current style, to the knees, and his knee stockings were made from some wool I had dyed to match his pants. His jacket was sleeveless, a dark heavy wool that I had made for him some years before. He had an orchid colored fall astor blossom on his lapel.

Capt. Stone came back with them to Gove's Ridge for the party that would follow their wedding. We had a Husking Bee in the Edgerly's barn; Capt. Stone played his fiddle; the Gove brothers happened to be on the Ridge, and they joined us for a glass of cider and gave their good wishes to Sim and Lib. We taught the Edgerly boys and the Tufts girls about an old-fashioned Husking Bee, and we got our corn husked, too.

For a few minutes, I allowed myself to have a short "If only." If only Henry were here to see his son and his son's lovely Bride. If Henry could only be as proud of Sim as I was!

After a pot-luck supper, for which I made the biggest Indian Pudding I could, we all went home. Capt. Stone stayed with the Edgerlys in their big house. Samuel Edgerly, who had given his room to Mr. Stone, came to sleep in our loft, and the bride and groom went to Sim's cabin. He was the happiest I've ever seen him. I watched to see if he would skip on his way home with his Lib. Dear Lib did the skipping, and Sim did the smiling, each enough for the two of them. A happier couple I've never seen.

Chapter 18

1794 - 1799

The five years between November of 1794 and December of 1799 slipped by on Gove's Ridge. My girls grew in size and knowledge. Their ways with the world remained similar to their toddler ways: each a little different.

My dear Deborah was serious about most things, seldom laughed or played jokes on her sisters, but she enjoyed grown-up talks with Sim and Lib about events in our daily lives in Limington. My Deb was proud of her weaving and other fiber crafts, which she worked very hard to get perfect. Like her younger sisters except little Catherine, she could plan and serve a meal, complete with something baked in the brick oven, and seemed to enjoy her turn to do so.

At the age of twelve, she was nearly as tall as I was. With her blue eyes and waves of light brown hair, my Deb was developing into a beautiful girl. She could read and write well, and was good at her arithmetic lessons. We practiced those with knitting that would fit a particular person or size.

She knew about planning socks, sweaters, and also blankets on the loom by figuring the number of stitches or threads per inch and then working from that. She held her breath each time she brought me a piece of knitting or showed me some weaving she had done on the loom. She wanted her craft work to please me, and she tried very hard to earn my praise. I was reminded of dear Pa Tufts when he looked at the things I had made to show him, and I remember how important it was to me to have his smile and nod of approval.

Hannah applied herself at the fiber skills by short spells. She bounced her way with joy through learning to read and write as well as the fiber craft work. At nearly ten years old, Hannah was growing tall, and with her bright blue eyes that crinkled in fun most of the time, and her straight hair in braids a shade darker than Deborah's, she had her own kind of beauty. She was always happy with a finished piece of work, and anxious for me to say she could go on to learn the next thing, even if what she presented for my approval wasn't quite right. She hated to be told to do it again. Like Deborah, Hannah read and wrote well. Arithmetic was her nightmare, and so her knitting was not any particular size. She had a very hard time memorizing the times tables. She loved to cook a meal, and always had an extra touch of flavor in her hotch potches because she liked to add herbs that were not the usual ones.

Nancy Ann seemed to have a natural bent for the fiber crafts. She did not appear to work terribly hard, but her work always looked very well done for her age of eight or so. She would smile her shy smile and say little as she progressed from one kind of craft work to the next. She often helped Hannah to finish a project such as a knitted sock, and she patiently showed both Hannah, who was older than she, and Catherine, who was younger than she, how to turn the heel of a sock, or how to thread the heddles of the loom for a project. Nancy Ann was my star pupil in the fiber crafts, and I had to be careful not to make her my all-round favorite daughter. She cooked "Because people have to eat," she said, and she was good, but not inspired, at cooking over the fireplace.

Nancy Ann's dark blue eyes and very light brown hair that curled a little around her face promised beauty to come a little later, when she had finished the years that I called "coltish," during the time she was all long legs that needed to be grown into. While the fiber crafts, including knitting to a size, were easy for Nancy Ann, learning to read and write were hard. She liked to do arithmetic problems, such as planning the turning of a heel of a sock, and she memorized the times tables easily. Reading and writing were not so easy for her.

My dear little Catherine remained small in size, but she was wise in her ways. Although she was only a few years old during these five years, it was plain to see that she noticed and learned from the mistakes made by her older sisters as she explored the ways of the world. She seldom got herself into big trouble with me, and so she was seldom punished. She was not a "Goody, Goody" girl, but she took advantage of her position of youngest in the family and she learned from it. Her fiber craft skills were average for her age, I thought. Her finished work was acceptable, but not outstanding. She worked very hard to get it that way. Nancy Ann was her biggest help and support, and Catherine always looked for her when she had questions about anything. Because of her size and age, I did not begin to teach her how to cook over the fireplace until she was about ten years old. Catherine's large and expressive blue eyes and her blonde curls made her a beauty. She did not seem to be aware of her good looks, however. She applied herself to her chapbook for reading and beginning to print, and she could spin yarn and knit a simple sock, with Nancy Ann's help with the arithmetic, by the time she was five years old.

As we settled into a routine on Gove's Ridge, I began to miss gathering for worship. During the years in Lee, I had been able to attend Sunday meetings for worship quite often. During the hard years with Mary Tufts, Sundays were a welcome respite. On Gove's Ridge, there was no meeting house where we could go. The nearest one, in Limington Center, was ten miles away. One day when I was visiting Sim and Lib in their cabin, I mentioned that I missed Bible reading and meetings to worship. "It means more to me than I had thought. I wonder what we can do about having a gathering once a week to read the Bible and talk about God."

They seemed to like that idea, and we decided to speak with Abby and Richard about it. The Edgerlys were in agreement, and said they would like their children to learn about our Lord, too.

From that time on, Sunday nights were for Bible study in my cabin. All the children were welcome, and we had treats like popped corn to string and munch to help them enjoy the meetings. In all, five adults—Sim and Lib, Abby and Richard, and I, were there. Often, there were also friends with us. We took turns choosing a Bible passage to read aloud to the group and then to talk about. We soon learned that Abby and Lib were good at making up a story to teach the lesson of the Bible passage to the children, who ranged from twelve years to babes in arms, as Lib and Abby added to their families. Lib and Abby were told each week what the next week's Bible Chapter would be, and so they took turns with their stories for the young ones.

After the Bible lesson, a Sunday night pot luck supper was always held to increase our fellowship. Each of the women brought a dish to share, and so a recipe swap was often part of the talk among the women. After supper, Sim and Richard and any men who might be visiting us, usually went to the porch to smoke their pipes, rock in the chairs, and talk about their current land clearing and farming chores, while the older children played tag or another game they called "dodge ball" near my porch. With the men and older children outside the cabin, the women often shared child-raising problems, or other concerns they might have while clearing up after the supper inside the cabin.

So, when my dear Deb seemed to be developing into a sassy, brassy, kind of young woman, I shared my concerns with Lib and Abby. "I can't seem to 'connect' with Deb like I used to. Whatever I talk about, she disagrees with. She will not follow directions in weaving or knitting, and often gets into messes that I have to straighten out for her, and she seems to resent my helping her out even in that way. She is not her old self, and I can't figure out why."

Both of my dear friends had noticed a change in Deborah, and promised to think about my concern for the next week. Both of them knew the story of my early life, and how my Aunt, whom Deborah was named after, had tried to guide me into a different life than I had chosen. The next time we talked about my Deb, they asked how old I was when I began to ignore my Aunt's advice. Of course, I was older—in my late twenties–when I met Henry, who turned my head so totally. None of us thought that Deb could have met a young man who might have as much influence on her as Henry had had on me, because none lived near enough for her to have met him. We decided to think about what could be done about her stubborn and unpleasant ways. I began to fear Mary Tufts' sickness in her head, but I never shared that dark thought with anyone.

Finally, it was decided that Simeon, the next time he went to Lee or to Northwood to see his uncle Thomas, would ask for advice and help with my Deborah. Sim came home with an invitation: "Deb, your brother Thomas has invited you to visit with him and his family in Lee. His wife is about to have their second child, and she could use your help with running the household, especially your good cooking. They can give you a room and your meals, and a few pence a week for your pocket, and you can see a different kind of living. Our Uncle Thomas will be your guardian, and you will have to answer to him for anything you do wrong."

My Deb clapped her hands. "Thank God! I've been praying for a place to go away from this dull Ridge! I'll start packing. Can you take me to Lee soon, Sim?"

"I'll take you within the week, Deb."

So, it was decided. She left us in the spring of 1797, when she was almost fifteen years old. I missed the old Deb after she was gone from us, but I did not miss the recent Deb at all. I knew that she would have a good life with Brother Thomas's guidance, if she would listen to it.

Meanwhile, the Ridge population was growing by leaps and bounds. Sim and Lib had their first son in January of 1796, and then another child, a girl, was born to them 1797, one in 1798, and another in 1799. They came so fast that I forgot their names, and I never remembered whether the new grandchild was a boy or a girl. I tried to caution Sim that Lib's bounce would not last through such rapid births, but nothing I said seemed to stop the new appearances.

Richard and Abby added two girls to their three boys, and so the little school in my cabin began to grow. I attended all the births, of course, and Abby helped with Lib's as Lib helped with Abby's. Fortunately, all the births were regular and so I could manage them.

After a year or so, Deb visited us on the Ridge, and later we received word that she had married a Jonathan Knowlton in Lee. When she returned to us, she was much more like her old self, and so I was glad for her.

My age began to show itself to me in the late 1790's, when my joints began to be painful and stiff, my teeth began to ache and then fall out, and my eyesight wouldn't let me weave the delicate linsey-woolsey patterns any more. If the heddles were threaded for me, I could work the shuttle, but I could no longer thread the loom. I knew it was time for me to slow down my pace a little. By 1799, Hannah was fourteen, Nancy Ann was ten, and little Catherine was seven. Hannah and Nancy Ann took turns with the planning of meals and the cooking of them. I could still teach them in the fiber crafts, especially knitting, and I could use the chapbooks for reading and writing and arithmetic because I could print them large enough for my tired eyes to see. One day Sim brought me a gift that he called "spectacles." "Put them on, Maw, with the circles over your ears to hold them in place. They should help you see better."

They did, and once more I could thread the heddles and weave! More and more I enjoyed my rocking chair on my front porch, especially in the evenings during the spring, summer, and fall months. The winters seemed to get colder and colder, and I enjoyed my rocker near my big fireplace during those months. There was always a "lap cat," often named "Cat'n Lap," to keep me company as I rocked and thought about many things. As the little Tufts "Grands" appeared every year, and the little Edgerlys, too, I seemed always to have good listeners for telling stories.

One of the children's favorite stories was about the first visit to my cabin by the Sokokis Indians, who went by twice each spring. Although I've forgotten, I think it was early the first spring I lived in my cabin, probably 1794, that I invited them to set up a camp in my front yard. They were on their way south from the White Mountains, that lay to the north and west where they had a winter camp, to "Salmon Rock" in the Saco River, they said. (That name is Indian, pronounced "Socko," and means "big fish River" they told me) The Goves had told us about them, said they were peaceful, and would not harm our animals or children. However, I had heard much about Indians since my childhood, I was very uneasy during their first visit.

I saw that the women wore very soft leather leggings and dresses below their knees. The men, who wore no "warpaint," also wore leggings and aprons, front and back. The men's front and back aprons and shirts were embroidered, as the women's dresses were, with beads and thin lines that I later learned were porcupine quills. The quills had often been dyed bright colors. One of the women, who wore a very fancy headdress, seemed to be in charge of the group of about fifteen or twenty youngish men and women. She always made the final decisions for the group. I approved of that. On their feet they wore moccasins that were made of heavy leather and the moccasins were also embroidered with beads and quills.

I offered them drinks of cool water from my well, and we talked, using a word now and then, but mostly using sign language. They were going to catch the salmon that would be coming up the Saco River to spawn, or lay their eggs. "Salmon Rock" was a large ledge that rose in the middle of the River, and the rapids on either side of it made the Salmon a sort of ladder to jump from pool to pool on their way up the River. Salmon Rock was a short day's trek south of my cabin. The Indians camped on the ledge called Salmon Rock, built fires there, and cleaned and smoked their year's supply of fish each spring. Since it was late in the day when they came, I invited them to stay that night and camp on my cleared cabin site, and they seemed pleased to do so. They built a fire and settled down for the night, asking me to sit and talk with them after they had eaten. I showed them my fibercrafts and they liked the blankets very much, noting the different weights. The knitted items did not seem to appeal to them. They promised to stop by on their way back to their regular campsite at Ossippee Lake in the White Mountains and barter, if I would, some smoked Salmon for some blankets. I liked that idea, and nodded my head "Yes." Their visits became an event each year that told me Spring was on the way. They became good bartering customers, and I liked smoked Salmon, too.

As the sun began to fall behind Isenglass Hill to the west, I always knew it was time for the little Tufts children—so many I couldn't keep names straight those days—to head for their cabin, along with the Edgerly boys and one girl—the younger girl too little yet to come for stories. All in all, life was good, I thought, and although I occasionally wondered "What if" I hadn't told Henry to get out of my life? I might have someone to rock and remember with me these evenings.

One evening, as the sun was glinting off Isenglass Hill in the late Fall of 1799, I was holding "Cat'nLap," and smoking my evening pipe. It might well be the last such quiet evening porch rock, I mused, as a "Killing Frost" was surely due, along with the first snow of the winter. Then it would be too cold to rock on my front porch. As I rocked and remembered, my eyes turned toward the Sokokis Trail to the south. My old eyes made out the figure of a man walking up the hill toward my cabin. As he came closer, I saw the tilt of his hat that was familiar. As he came nearer, I saw the funny, familiar swing of his left leg as he walked; I knew who it was. A thousand feelings came and went in my heart. Resentment for all the difficult times he had made for me; Relief that he was still alive; Surprise that he was so near to finding me; Pleasure that he was alone; those were a few of the many things that came into my mind. My heart did a couple of cartwheels after missing a beat or two. My Henry was coming up the Sokokis Trail toward my cabin! When my mind had cleared enough for me to make a plan or two, I decided that he would not be welcome to stay with me, but at least I could re-heat some of our supper soup before I sent him on to Richard's or to Simeon's for the night that was coming on. Richard's would probably be better, because they knew him only from what they had heard about him, not from direct contact.

I sat and rocked until he came near enough for me to hear his heavy breathing, and his words, "Lyd, Lyd, is that you? Let me see if your eyes are still that cerulean hue. I have so much to tell you. May I come up and rock and stay awhile?"

Chapter 19

1799 – 1807

"Well, Henry. So, you've found us. How long have you been looking?"

"I've been looking for a long time, Lyd. I need to tell you some things. I have learned that I won't live forever, and that I have not always been a good husband to you. I want you to know that I've changed, and that I want to live only with you and be a proper husband to you. I also want to make up for my actions to our children."

"We'll see about that, Henry. There will be some conditions for you to meet if you want to live on our Ridge here in Limington. Richard and Sim will have a lot to say about that, I know. How did you find us?"

"I stopped by the old house in Lee and met our son, Thomas, and our beautiful daughter, Deborah. She is very popular with the young men of Lee. I expect there will be a wedding before long. Thomas is starting a family, too, and didn't seem to know me. I wonder why."

"Have you had your supper yet? We have some warm soup that you can have if you want it."

"I would like that, Lydia. Tell me, what are these 'conditions' you talk about?"

"They will all come out in time, Henry. Now, I'll get your soup and then you can go on to Richard and Abby's. There is no room for you to stay here in my cabin. I still have three girls to finish raising, you know. You sit right here and I'll bring you your soup."

I was not ready for Henry to check the inside of my cabin, and so I wanted him to stay on the porch. He did.

"My, this is good, Lydia. I had forgotten what a good cook you are!"

"My Hannah made the soup, Henry. She is a good cook, if I say so myself, and I taught her how."

"Where is she now, Lyd?"

"She and Nancy Ann are at a neighbor's Frolic here in Limington. Catherine is helping Lib at Sim's cabin with their newest babe, who has the colic."

As soon as Henry had finished his soup, I pointed out the path to Richard and Abby's. He went slowly on his way, seeming surprised at my not asking him to stay with me. I had talked with Richard and Abby about Henry's palaver, and so they would listen to, but not believe, much he said. I was tired when he had gone, but a little relieved, I had to admit to myself, that he was still alive. I left the lantern lighted and hanging on the porch for the girls to see to put the horse—a younger one than Kit named Jetty—and the wagon away.

It had been a long time since I had thought of my father's advice to ". . .stand up straight and BE somebody," in the face of difficult times, but I thought of those words as I went to sleep that night. Tomorrow would be a time I'd need to remember them well, because we would be dealing with Henry Tufts, the well known horse thief, jail escaper, liar and womanizer.

Early the next morning, Sim, Richard, and Henry arrived at my cabin.

"Time for a family talk," said Sim.

I invited Sim and Richard inside, and we spoke in low tones so as not to wake the girls, who were still asleep in the loft above. As we gathered around the table Sim had made for me, I told Sim and Richard what I had said to Henry the night before. They were glad that I had not invited him to stay with me. They urged me not to do so while the girls were still with me. I agreed to that, remembering brother Thomas's wife's reaction to Henry's ways so long ago in Northwood. Richard said,

"I can fix a small room for Henry in our carriage shed. It will be fine during the summer, and this winter I'll fix a stove for him to use."

Sim liked that idea, and I agreed. Then, we talked about feeding Henry. Sim and Richard were determined that he find work to pay for his food as well as his room at Richard and Abby's. Sim would take his father, whom he called, "Hen," to meet the Town's Selectmen, men who were elected by the voters to run the day-to-day business of the Town. Sim said, "I know they've been looking for a Highway Surveyor to keep records of the number of hours different men work on cutting brush and other kinds of road work. I think it pays pretty well. I can see that Hen has an axe to cut brush, and among us we can see that he goes to work every day. Do you think that will keep him on the straight and narrow?"

We agreed that it would be worth a try. I thought that I could feed him for thirty cents a day, and Richard said they would collect a dollar a week for his room. Sim and Richard thought Hen could earn at least five dollars a week, if he tended to his job. We decided it would be best to collect the money from him <u>in advance.</u> The next thing we had to do was inform Henry of the conditions he would have to meet to live with us on our Ridge. We decided that he would not think our conditions fair, but Hen didn't think that anything that required him to walk a straight line was fair, anyway.

Sim, Richard, and I went out to my porch to talk with Henry. As we laid out the conditions he would need to meet, he began to wheedle and try to get me, especially, to give way. I stayed the course, and Sim and Richard supported me all the way as we talked. Sim summed up our conditions for Henry: "That's how it is, Hen. If you want to live here on Gove's Ridge with us, you'll earn your keep. You'll work every day, and you'll pay for the things you need. You haven't done that in the past, and we know that for a fact. Now things will be different. Otherwise, you know the way down the Sokokis Trail to Waterborough and beyond. Mother Tufts got along without you in all the past years, she raised five of your children by herself, and she can get along for the rest of her life without you in it. It's as plain as that!"

That was a very long speech for my Sim, but he had said it all right out loud! I was proud of him, and I thanked him many times for it during the next years.

As Sim and Richard walked up the path toward their cabins, with Henry between them, I made a picture in my mind that I remembered for a long time. My two young, strong upright tall men had Henry shoulder–to- shoulder between them. He would have to be very foxy if he found a way to stray off the straight and narrow path now, I thought.

Later that day, I watched as Sim and Richard, with Henry riding on the top, took a large load of logs on a sledge down the Trail toward Nason's Mill. They would go about five miles down the Little Ossippee River to the Mill, where the logs the boys had cut off their land would be sawed into boards and then stacked to dry for the winter. The next spring, the boards would be ready for some building or other they had planned, I was sure. Henry would either have to work for the Town or else work with Sim and Richard clearing their land. I was sure Henry would choose working for the Town rather than lumbering with my boys. Clearing the land was hard labor, and Henry was not used to that.

Nancy Ann and Hannah roused from sleep late that morning. They'd had a wonderful time at the Frolic, and Hannah had a good time teasing

Nancy Ann about the young man with curly red hair who was making eyes at her. Nancy Ann just smiled her little smile and said nothing. She was a quiet one! While the girls ate their breakfast, I told them about their father's arrival. I tried not to picture him in a very bad light, but I felt that I had to be honest. I told them about some of his shenanigans, and warned them not to be taken in by his stories. They each reacted in a typical way. Hannah laughed and Nancy Ann looked a little sad at the things I told them.

Our lives continued on, and 1799 became 1800. Another baby, named Sarah, joined Lib and Sim. A baby girl named Sarah had joined Abby and Richard the past September of 1799. That May of 1800, I became fifty eight, Catherine turned just eight, Hannah became prettier at fifteen, Nancy Ann became eleven, and Henry reached fifty-two. At his age, Hen acted less of an adult than his son, Simeon, who was thirty one and Richard, who was thirty eight. The seasonal work went on, and it became more farm work and less land-clearing. That was welcome to Sim and Richard, I was sure.

Sim and Richard kept me aware of the local news, and public schools were being talked of for the Town of Limington. Teachers would be paid from taxpayers' money. Sim quickly registered those of his brood who would be old enough to attend school in a year or so, as did Richard. There was also talk of a Church to be established near the Post Office-General Store in South Limington. That would be about 5 miles from us, — not as far to go with a horse and wagon as

Limington Center, where the first Church in town was built. That was good, because the Sunday night worship services we had been having soon grew boring for the children who did not like Henry's "New Light" preaching. They also did not like his trying to get us all to do religious dancing like the Shakers, whom he had visited in Alfred on some of his jaunts. Life changed with Henry around, but it did not get dull, that's for sure.

We received word of Deborah's marriage to Jonathan Knowlton in August of 1801. Sim learned from his brother Thomas that it was a small wedding in Lee, and the Bride and Groom soon set out for Farmington, Maine, where they lived out their lives.

My happy Hannah took Deborah's place and went to live with her older brother, Thomas, in Lee, to help with his growing family. I missed her terribly, and she must have missed us, too, because she came to Limington whenever she could arrange it. She told us of Irish Hannah, for whom she was named, and she told me the Irish girls, Hannah and Nancy, were doing well although getting older. I sent word to them to come and visit us on our ever-growing Ridge.

My baby, Catherine, turned ten in 1802, and I began to teach her to cook. She was old enough and big enough by then to work safely around the fireplace. She became a good cook, and she especially liked to bake things in the brick oven. One of her specialties was baked beans. She knew how to add molasses, spices, and even an onion and a piece of bacon to make the beans taste very good. Then, she let them bake slowly in the brick oven until they melted in my mouth.

Hannah did not marry until after Nancy Ann, who married a Limington young man in 1810, when she was twenty-one. My dear Nancy Ann settled down near enough so that I saw her more often than I saw the other girls, and I began to look forward very much to her visits. We talked and talked about the fiber crafts, which I loved. Nancy Ann was very good at all the crafts I enjoyed so much. She earned some money now and then with her knitting and weaving.

Richard and I took the pay for Henry's room and meals in advance as planned, thinking that would keep him in one place–for the most part. However, he was very restless, and found a pattern for his life so that he would work, usually for the Town of Limington, either as Highway Surveyor or doctoring the poor, long enough to buy his room and board for a month or so ahead, and then disappear for a few weeks. Sometimes he shared with us where he said he had been, and often he didn't. As long as he paid his bills, we didn't show much interest in his absences.

One day in December of 1807, he came to my cabin waving, with a book in his hand and a big smile on his face.

"See, Lydia, what I have done! I wrote a book, a real book, and it was printed in Dover! This copy is for you."

He handed me a small book titled, A NARRATIVE OF THE ADVENTURES, TRAVELS, AND SUFFERINGS OF HENRY TUFTS, NOW RESIDING AT LEMINGTON IN THE DISTRICT OF MAINE.

Chapter 20

1808 – 1834

Henry told everyone, of course, about his book. Before long, in early March of 1808, Sim and I were called to Lee by Henry's brothers Thomas and Eliphalet. They, along with young Thomas, were very angry over Henry's book and they wanted a family meeting to talk about it. So we took Sim's new Surrey with his fastest horse and made the trip. It was surely faster than the trek we had made when we moved to the Ridge in 1793. We needed to stay one night in Lee. Richard and Abby said they would take care of our animals, as well as Henry, while we were gone.

The Lee relatives were very upset that the book had so many lies in it, they said, and the book was not, probably, written by Henry, but rather by another person. The flowery and "high falutin' language were not Henry's way of talking, and so they doubted he wrote it. They wondered what Sim and I were going to do about the terrible book that showed such a bad picture of our family.

I told them that for many years, Sim and I had been the very helpless victims of Henry, but we had found our own ways to overcome that and to protect ourselves from his lies, connivings, and thieveries. Among other things, I told them how I handled Henry's habit of stealing money from the till in the Tailor Shop during Pa's lifetime. These days on the Ridge, we were getting along with him and accepting most of his ways that did no injury to us or anyone near us. We had not considered doing anything about the book. It couldn't hurt us we had agreed, when Sim and I talked on our way south to Lee.

We tried to make our position clear to those family members, and they seemed to accept our way of dealing with Henry. They were respectful, but decided to differ, as it turned out.

I was so glad to see my dear Hannah again, as well as the Irish Hannah and Nancy. The four of us had happy talks, in contrast to the anger in the talks Sim and I had with Henry's brothers and son. The next day, we returned sad, but not angry, to our Ridge homes in Limington.

As we traveled at a good pace toward home, we talked about Henry's bad habits, and how he used everyone, even his close relatives, so badly. We decided that our present treatment, which did not shame him, but prevented him from hurting anyone else, was the best we could do. As long as any of my girls lived with me, I would not have him live with me too. I fed him three good meals a day, but then he went to Richard's carriage shed to sleep.

Lib and Simeon continued adding to their family. A girl named Salome joined them in 1808, a little boy with the big name of Thomas Jefferson Tufts was born in August, 1810, another little boy born in 1815 did not live long, then a boy arrived in May of 1818. His name was Charles Alonzo Tufts. He was their last child. There was another boy in there somewhere, named William, but I'm not sure of his birth date. As I had feared, the rapid births had sapped dear Lib's strength, and she was never the bouncy, happy woman we had all come to love. Sim was his sober, kind, and patient self throughout her entire life.

The years passed, and our Hannah got word to us that she had married a Massachusetts man in 1811. She and her husband, named George Miller, came to see us in Limington only once that I remember. He was a nice enough man, but she was not "mine" any more. They finally settled in Portland, Maine, I was told.

Henry came and went, as usual. He was always careful to pay his expenses ahead of time. He earned money from the Town of Limington with his "Doctoring," and was proud of a receipt he had given the town for payment of $25.00 to him for care of a town "charge," another name for pauper. He also worked on the roads as Highway Surveyor. After one of Henry's treks, he told us he had visited Deborah and her family in Farmington, a town quite far to the north. He said he had found Deborah a handsome woman, whom he was proud to call "my daughter." I wondered how proud she was to have Henry do that, and if she had heard about his book.

My dear Catherine stayed small for her age, but she had many good talents. Her fiber craft work came along well, and she became an expert cook at the fireplace. Her baked beans and Indian pudding were always very popular at Frolics. She was eighteen in 1820, and she introduced me to Mr. George Conant, whom she said she intended to marry. The winter flu was very bad during those years, and he did not live very long—only about two years—before he caught the flu and died. There were no children and she came back to my cabin to live. Before long, she married again, to Jonathan Whiting, and they lived not far away in Limington.

In 1820, Maine was named a State of the United States, and Limington became a Town within the State of Maine. We no longer lived in the "Northern Province." About a year before we moved to the Ridge, it was no longer considered to be in the "Ossipee Plantation," because the Town of Limington had been formed. We were becoming more and more a part of the United States of America. I thought about the changes I had seen in our lives—from fearing Indian raids and privateer attacks from the ocean, to being part of a town and a now part of a state. Changes, changes.

By 1825, the Sokokis Indians were no longer making their spring treks to the Saco for salmon. Other than birthings and some care of the sick, I was not very busy. I had given up raising flax, because the process of making thread was long and very tiring. Besides, I did not like to look at the hatchel, where my second baby, Thomas, had nearly died. Next, I stopped working with fleece. Sim and

Richard had a friend who sheared their sheep for them. After the shearing they took the fleeces to the mill for cleaning, carding, and dyeing. I always kept my spinning wheel and loom ready to go, and I knitted warm sweaters, caps, and mittens, but I did not worry about "production" those days.

Gradually, when my eyes would allow, I had read Henry's book. I had to agree with the Lee family members. It was full of lies, and the words in the book were not Henry's. The poetry it contained did not seem to really belong to him, except for one short poem that I noticed. He was describing my talking to him about his conduct after he came to live on the Ridge:

"Women, like men, will fade away,
Their eyes grow dim, their teeth decay,
But while they breathe the vital gale,
'Tis strange their tongue should never fail." (1)

"Well," I smiled to myself, "at least something has penetrated his skull, and he has heard some of my scolding about the things he does."

As Lib's strength grew less and less, I found myself at Sim's cabin to help with the children much of the time. Sometimes it was easier for Lib if I took some of the older children to my cabin. It was a little nearer to their schoolhouse in South Limington, too. I enjoyed getting to know them all, because they all had different ways about them. I showed the girls about cooking with a fireplace and brick oven, and some of the boys liked to weave on the big old loom and spin with the walking wheel.

More and more, I enjoyed my rocking chair on my front porch in the evening. There was always "Cat'n'Lap" to rock with me, and even without any teeth, my pipe was a pleasure. I still had a good supply of my favorite tobacco the Indians had told me how to raise. Rocking made my back ache less, and the pains in my shoulders and knees felt better after a good rock, too. Using the feelings in my old body, I began to be able to predict the weather. I knew when we would get a storm, whether rain in spring, summer, and fall or snow in winter. My fireplace was a comfort in the cold, and so the rocking chair was moved into the living room. Richard and Sim were my blessings for such tasks, and I seldom had to ask them to do something—they seemed to know what I needed. My animals had been reduced to one cow, one pig, and some hens and a rooster. Sim and/or Richard or one of their big boys often tended to the animals when I couldn't get around very well. Between them, Sim and Richard and their boys kept me supplied with feed and water for the few animals I had left, and they also brought wood for my fire and water to use. They took me anywhere I needed to go. One day, I thought how lucky my old age was. After the years of uncertainty and going without things I needed, here I was, so well cared for. There was not a thing I could even wish for. I knew that when I was finished with my cabin it would be Richard's property, because it was built on his land. I didn't mind that. Richard and Abby had been like a son and daughter to me for all these years on Gove's Ridge.

The winter of 1830-1831 was a hard one to forget. Snow came early in November, and remained covering the ground until late April. "An old-fashioned winter," folks called it. By December first, Lib was sick in bed with the flu, and her cough was a wracking one. Nothing that I could think of to do would help it. I stewed onions, molasses and ginger for cough syrup, made Ipecac tea to help her raise the phlegm, and I rendered chicken fat to rub on her chest. I did all the things I knew how to do. She died on December twenty-second. Her services were held in the South Limington meeting house, and her body was put into the tomb there until spring. That was the custom then, because digging a grave in the frozen ground was impossible. She was deeply mourned and missed by everyone.

Simeon asked to have his children near to him during his first weeks without Lib, and so my cabin was empty again. One day he came to me, with concern on his face and in his eyes.

"Mother, I hate to ask you to do this, but Hen is in bad shape with the flu. Richard and Abby cannot care for him, and I don't want him to give the flu to my family. Can you take him in here and care for him? Abby and Richard and I'll be glad to see that you have everything you need, including your food. He's in very bad shape, or I wouldn't ask you to do this."

"Of course, Sim. I'll take care of Henry. I've always known that I would see him through to the end, one way or another. I'd appreciate all of you helping with our food, too. That's kind of you."

Henry had the same sounding cough that Lib had had. I did the same for him. I made a cough syrup of onions, molasses, with a little ginger in it, but that did not do much. I got out the Ipecac, but that did not touch his phlegm. I rubbed his chest with hen's fat, and made a poultice with hot cloths. That seemed to help a little for a while. During one of the times he was awake, he asked me,

"Lyd, I've been a good husband, in the end, haven't I?"

"You've done your best, Henry, now rest."

Henry died January twenty-one, 1831. It was less than a month after we had lost our dear Lib. Many described Henry's death as coming "after a sadly misspent life."

There was no funeral for Henry, one had been scheduled, but there was a blizzard instead. No one could have attended, so his body was put into the same vault as Lib's to await burial in the spring.

Simeon and Richard saw to it that Lib and Henry received proper burials in the spring of 1831. Life on the Ridge in Limington changed without them. I missed dear Lib terribly. I knew that Abby missed her, too. She was always a cheerful presence at our gatherings and Frolics. I knew that Simeon missed her terribly, and I began to suspect that he was looking for someone to fill his empty heart. Finally, he brought Lucy Hasty to meet me. I liked her, and told Sim that I did. However, I cautioned him that, at sixty one, he should not look for more than a companion for his late years. He seemed to listen carefully.

There was not a wedding in my lifetime, so he heeded my words, I think. Lucy remained his housekeeper as long as I was aware of the world.

As for missing Henry, I did not. It was as if a heavy load had been lifted from my mind and heart. I had done my best to fulfill my wedding vows to Henry, and I had done my best to fulfill my duty to our children. All of the children were alive and thriving. They had all married, and were productive, good citizens, living uprightly. I said a little prayer of thanks each time I thought about them. I had gone against my elders' advice, and in spite of difficulties, I had completed my tasks through the life I had chosen. I was at peace with myself, with my God, and with the world.

As August of 1834 approached, I knew there would not be a winter time again for me. I began to have a heavy feeling in my chest, and sometimes when I lay down in my bed, I had a hard time to breathe. Someone was always with me these days in case I needed anything, but I needed little. Sleep was my friend.

(1) p. 341, Edmund Pearson.

Post Script

Lydia died in her sleep in mid-August, 1834. She was ninety-two years, 3 months old. Simeon married Lucy Hasty in December, 1834. Lydia left a legacy of descendents, one of whom was Grandson Simeon Stone Tufts, who left Gove's Ridge for a time to work on the Erie Canal in New York state. He returned to live out his life on the Ridge. His son served in the Civil War, some descendents served in WWI, and several more served our country in WWII.

For More Information

BOOKS

Fitts, Rev. James Hill, A History of Newfields, N. H., 1638 –1911, Concord, N.H., 1912.

George, Nellie Palmer, Old Newmarket, N.H., News-Letter Press, Exeter, N.H., 1932.

Getchell, Sylvia Fitts, The Tide Turns On The Lamprey, A History of Newarket, N.H., Priv. Pub., 1984.

Goodwin, Del & Dorcas Chaffee, Eds., Perspectives '76, N. H. & VT. Ed.

Resources Program, Hanover, H. N., 1975.

Hamilton, Charles, Ed., Men of the Underworld, the Professional Criminals' Own Story, The MacMillan Co., 1952.

Hill, Ralph Nading, Yankee Kingdon: Vermont and New Hampshire, Harper Brothers, New York,1960.

Pearson, Edmond, Queer Books, Doubleday & Co., N. Y., 1928.

_____, Ed., Autobiography Of A Criminal, Henry Tufts, Duffield and Co., New York, 1930.

Scales, John, History of Strafford County, N. H. & Representative Citizens, Richmond- Arnold Pub. Co., Chicago, 1914.

Taylor, Robert, Early Families of Limington, Maine, Heritage Books, Maryland, 1991.

MAGAZINES

Helfrich, G. W., "An Uncommonly Misspent Life," Down East Magazine, November, 1989.

Parks, Julie & Chris Clarke, "Legend Lore", Upcountry, November, 1985.

Stevens, Jay, "Confessions of Professional Black Sheep", Yankee Magazine, Dublin, N. H., 1986.

INTERNET

New England Historic Genealogical Society website NewEnglandAncestors.Org, 2010

Shirley Durgin was born on her father's family farm in Limington, Maine, in 1928. After elementary schools in Limington and Limerick, she graduated from Berwick Academy, Class Salutatorian, in 1946. In 1951 she married Ted Nelson. After their two children were in school, she began to take college courses, and in 1965 received a BA in Education, Magna Cum Laude, from Lesley College. After more than 20 years teaching Language Arts in several schools and at several levels in Massachusetts and Vermont, she and Ted began to spend winters in Frostproof, Florida. Early in the 1990s, Shirley joined The Knitters Guild of America and was named a Master Knitter and a Certified Teacher of Knitting by 1994. Since March of 2006, they have lived at Florida Presbyterian Homes, a retirement community in Lakeland, Florida.